THE ULTIMATE AIR FRYER COOKBOOK

Healthy, Crispy, and Delicious Recipes to Cook Every Meal with Ease | Full Color Edition

Amy G. Mattison

Copyright© 2025 By Amy G. Mattison Rights Reserved

This book is copyright protected. It is only for personal use. You cannot amend, distribute, sell, use, quote or paraphrase any part of the content within this book, without the consent of the author or publisher.

Under no circumstances will any blame or legal responsibility be held against the publisher, or author, for any damages, reparation, or monetary loss due to the information contained within this book, either directly or indirectly.

Limit of Liability/Disclaimer of Warranty:

No book, including this one, can ever replace the diagnostic expertise and medical advice of a physician in providing information about your health. The information contained herein is not intended to replace medical advice. You should consult with your doctor before using the information in this or any health-related book.

The Publisher and the author make no representations or warranties with respect to the accuracy or completeness of the contents of this work and specifically disclaim all warranties, including without limitation warranties of fitness for a particular purpose. No warranty may be created or extended by sales or promotional materials. The advice and strategies contained herein may not be suitable for every situation. This work is sold with the understanding that the Publisher is not engaged in rendering medical, legal, or other professional advice or services. If professional assistance is required, the services of a competent professional person should be sought. Neither the Publisher nor the author shall be liable for damages arising here from. The fact that an individual, organization, or website is referred to in this work as a citation and/or potential source of further information does not mean that the author or the Publisher endorses the information the individual, organization, or website may provide or recommendations they/it may make. Further, readers should be aware that websites listed in this work may have changed or disappeared between when this work was written and when it is read.

Manufactured in the United States of America
Interior and Cover Designer: Danielle Rees
Art Producer: Brooke White
Editor: Aaliyah Lyons
Production Editor: Sienna Adams
Production Manager: Sarah Johnson
Photography: Michael Smith

TABLE OF CONTENTS

Introduction 1

Chapter 1: Welcome to the Air Fryer Revolution 2

    Getting to Know Your Air Fryer 2

    The Benefits of the Air Fryer 3

    Tips for Air Fryer Beginners 4

    Air Fryer Cooking Chart 6

Chapter 2: Appetizers and Small Bites 8

    Cheesy Broccoli Bites 9

    Ham and Cheese Spinach Dip 9

    Roasted Ranch Chickpeas 10

    Classic French Fries 10

    Salmon Nachos 11

    Puff Pastry-Wrapped Cocktail Sausages 11

    Crispy Fried Pickles 12

    Crispy Kale Chips with Tex-Mex Dip 12

    Roasted Grape and Basil Dip 13

    Spicy Sweet Potato Fries 13

    Shrimp Toasts 14

    Asian Vegetable Pot Stickers 14

Chapter 3: Breakfast Favorites 15

TABLE OF CONTENTS

Meatless Breakfast Sausage 16

Cheese Omelette 16

Scrambled Pancake Hash 17

Fresh Raspberry Scones 17

Breakfast Chicken Strips 18

Herbed Breakfast Eggs 18

Italian Breakfast Frittata 19

Breakfast Tuna & Bacon 19

Gourmet Grilled Cheese 20

Cheesy Puff Pastry Egg Tarts 20

Veggie & Cheese Egg Cups 21

Pecan Rolled Oat Granola 21

Chapter 4: Poultry Dishes 22

Easy Chicken Nuggets 23

BBQ Turkey Breasts 23

Chicken Cordon Bleu 24

Ham and Cheese Stuffed Chicken 24

Turkey and Avocado Sliders 25

Old Bay Crispy Chicken Wings 25

Turkey Sausage Patties 26

Teriyaki Chicken Kebabs 26

Chicken Meatballs 27

TABLE OF CONTENTS

Parmesan Crusted Chicken Fillet 27

Hot & Spicy Buffalo Wings 28

Authentic Chicken Fajitas 28

Chapter 5: Meat Recipes 29

Rosemary Ribeye Steak 30

Beef Shoulder with Onion 30

Tenderloin Steaks with Mushrooms 31

Herb Butter Steak 31

BBQ Pork Chops 32

Beef Roll-Up 32

Breaded Pork Cutlets 33

Sticky Bacon with Cauliflower 33

Classic Beef Pot Roast 34

Juicy Seasoned Pork Tenderloin 34

Chapter 6: Fish and Seafood Creations 35

Greek Fish Pita 36

Fried Fish Fingers 36

Crispy Salmon Sticks 37

Classic Fish Burgers 37

Crunchy Fish Taco 38

Tuna Wraps 38

Quick Shrimp Scampi 39

TABLE OF CONTENTS

Trout and Mint Mix 39

Lemon-Dill Salmon Burgers 40

Coconut Shrimp 40

Chapter 7: Side Dishes and Snacks 41

Mediterranean-Style Beet Chips 42

Classic Onion Rings 42

Tomato-Caprese Cups 43

Spiced Nuts 43

Cheese Bacon-Stuffed Mushrooms 44

Broccoli with Cheese & Olives 44

Garlic & Ginger Snow Peas 45

Artichoke Balls 45

Parmesan Asparagus Fries 46

Crispy Zucchini Fries 46

Cheddar-Olive Nuggets 47

Spicy and Sticky Brussels Sprouts 47

Chapter 8: Vegan and Vegetarian Meals 48

Hot Spicy Falafel 49

Creamed Spinach 49

Smashed Fried Baby Potatoes 50

Roasted Stuffed Peppers 50

Lemon Garlicky Cabbage 51

TABLE OF CONTENTS

Greek-Style Vegan Burgers 51

Chile-Cheese Cornbread with Corn 52

Fried Green Tomatoes 52

Crispy Baked Green Beans 53

Rosemary & Cheese-Roasted Red Potatoes 53

Herb-Roasted Vegetables 54

Breaded Zucchini Slices 54

Chapter 9: Delicious Desserts 55

Pumpkin Pie Roll-Ups 56

Bananas Foster 56

Grilled Plantain Boats 57

Blueberry-Cream Cheese Bread Pudding 57

Mini Monkey Rolls 58

Dark Chocolate Oatmeal Cookies 58

S'mores Pockets 59

Easy Fudge Brownie 59

Glazed Cherry Turnovers 60

Appendix 1: Measurement Conversion Chart 61

Appendix 2: The Dirty Dozen and Clean Fifteen 62

Appendix 3: Index 63

INTRODUCTION

The first time I tried the air fryer, I had no idea what I was doing. I had heard so much about how it could make everything from crispy fries to juicy chicken, but when I plugged it in, I had no clue what settings to use. I threw some frozen chicken nuggets in, set the temperature to what I thought was right, and walked away. Fifteen minutes later, I came back to a kitchen that smelled like burnt cardboard.

My 10-year-old son, always eager to get involved, walked in just as I was trying to salvage what was left. He looked at me, then at the pile of crispy, slightly overdone nuggets, and said, "Mom, I think we need to read the instructions next time."

Since then, the air fryer has become our kitchen companion. Now, it's not only my quick fix for busy days, but also a fun bonding experience with my son. He loves putting in his own snacks—like making little pizza rolls or crispy bacon—and watching it cook. It's amazing how something as simple as an air fryer has turned into a way for us to spend time together, cooking healthy meals without the stress or mess of traditional cooking. It's become a kitchen win for our family!

DEDICATION

James, my love son, I just want to take a moment to thank you. Your intelligence and daring spirit helped me figure out the air fryer, and I couldn't have done it without you. Your curiosity and willingness to jump in made all the difference when I was learning how to use it properly. You've also worked hard, helping me with so many chores, and it means so much. But what really makes me proud is when you became my little helper in the kitchen. Seeing your face light up as we cook together fills my heart.

CHAPTER 1: WELCOME TO THE AIR FRYER REVOLUTION

GETTING TO KNOW YOUR AIR FRYER

When you first unbox your air fryer, it can feel a bit overwhelming with all its buttons, dials, and features. However, understanding the basics will make using it second nature in no time. At its core, the air fryer is essentially a mini convection oven. It uses hot air circulation to cook food quickly and evenly, achieving that crispy texture we all love without needing much—if any—oil.

The key parts of the air fryer include the basket, drip tray, control panel, and heating element. The basket holds your food while it cooks, and the drip tray catches any excess grease or liquid that may drip from the food. The control panel is where you adjust the temperature, time, and cooking settings. Some models offer presets for specific foods, like fries or chicken, making them user-friendly for beginners. The heating element, usually located at the top of the unit, provides the necessary heat to cook and crisp the food.

Air fryers also use a fan to circulate the hot air, which is why you'll hear a slight humming sound while it's running. This air circulation is what allows the air fryer to cook food so quickly and uniformly. Familiarizing yourself with these parts will help you understand how the machine works and how to maintain it properly.

CHOOSING THE RIGHT MODEL FOR YOU

There are several types of air fryers available on the market, and selecting the right one can depend on a few factors, including your kitchen space, how often you'll use it, and your cooking style.

BASKET-STYLE AIR FRYERS

These are the most common models and typically feature a pull-out drawer that holds the food. They're compact, easy to use, and work well for small to medium batches. If you're cooking for a family of two or three, this style might be ideal for you. They're also the most budget-friendly option.

OVEN-STYLE AIR FRYERS

If you cook larger meals or need more versatility, an oven-style air fryer might be a better fit. These models often have multiple racks, allowing you to cook different foods at once, and sometimes even feature additional functions like baking, broiling, and toasting. They are larger and can take up more counter space, but their added features may make them worth the investment.

AIR FRYER TOASTER OVENS

These combine the best of both worlds—offering air frying capabilities along with traditional toaster

WELCOME TO THE AIR FRYER REVOLUTION

oven features. They are great for people who want an all-in-one kitchen appliance that can handle everything from air frying to roasting and baking.

When choosing your air fryer, consider the capacity. If you're cooking for a family or meal prepping, look for one with a larger capacity—something around 5-6 quarts. If you're cooking for one or two, a smaller capacity (around 2-4 quarts) will suffice.

Other features to look for include temperature range (a wider range gives you more flexibility), presets (for beginners, presets can simplify cooking), and ease of cleaning. Some models have non-stick baskets that are dishwasher safe, which is a huge time-saver.

SETTING UP FOR SUCCESS

Now that you've chosen your air fryer and unboxed it, it's time to get started! Before using your new appliance, it's important to give it a quick cleaning. Wash the basket and drip tray with warm, soapy water and dry them thoroughly. Wipe down the exterior and interior with a damp cloth to remove any dust from shipping.

Next, familiarize yourself with the control panel. Many air fryers have simple controls, usually a dial or digital display where you can set the temperature and cooking time. Some models also have preset options for specific foods. If your air fryer has presets, read the manual to understand how they work.

For your first few cooking attempts, keep it simple. Try making something like frozen fries or chicken nuggets to get a feel for how it works. Don't overcrowd the basket—air circulation is key to getting that crispy texture, so leave some space between the pieces. If you're cooking a larger batch, you may need to shake or flip the food halfway through to ensure even cooking.

Finally, remember that air fryers are quick, but every model is slightly different. It may take some experimentation to get the timing and temperature just right for your favorite foods. Don't be discouraged if things aren't perfect on the first try. The more you use your air fryer, the more intuitive it will become.

By taking the time to familiarize yourself with the basics of your air fryer, choosing the right model, and setting it up properly, you'll be on your way to creating delicious, healthy meals in no time.

THE BENEFITS OF THE AIR FRYER

The air fryer has become a must-have kitchen appliance, and for good reason. Its ability to create crispy, delicious meals with minimal oil, along with the convenience and versatility it offers, makes it a game-changer for busy families and anyone looking to cook healthier without sacrificing taste. Let's take a closer look at some of the top benefits of using an air fryer.

HEALTHIER MEALS, LESS OIL

One of the biggest draws of the air fryer is its ability to cook foods that are typically deep-fried using little to no oil. Traditional deep frying can add a significant amount of fat and calories to your meals, but the air fryer uses hot air circulation to crisp up food, providing the same texture and taste without the excess oil.

In fact, many air fryer recipes call for just a light spray or brush of oil—sometimes none at all! This significantly reduces the amount of fat in your meals. For example, if you were to make a batch of homemade French fries, you'd typically need a few cups of oil to fry them. In the air fryer, just a

CHAPTER 1

tablespoon or two is enough to achieve that golden, crispy exterior while keeping the inside tender and fluffy.

This reduction in oil means you can indulge in some of your favorite comfort foods like fries, chicken wings, or even doughnuts, but with fewer calories and less fat. And the best part? You won't feel like you're missing out on flavor or texture. The air fryer's hot air circulation ensures that the food is crispy, juicy, and full of flavor—just like it's been deep-fried, but healthier.

QUICK & CONVENIENT

If you're like most people, you're constantly juggling work, family, and home responsibilities, which can make finding time to cook a real challenge. The air fryer is here to help. It offers fast cooking times that allow you to prepare meals quickly, even on your busiest days.

Because the air fryer works by circulating hot air around the food, it cooks meals much faster than traditional ovens. For example, frozen chicken tenders that might take 20-25 minutes in the oven could be ready in just 12-15 minutes in the air fryer. Similarly, cooking frozen vegetables or French fries takes just a fraction of the time it would in a conventional oven, meaning you can spend less time in the kitchen and more time doing the things you love.

Another time-saving benefit of the air fryer is the easy cleanup. Since the appliance uses so little oil, you won't be left with a greasy mess to clean up afterward. Most air fryer baskets and trays are non-stick and dishwasher-safe, making them a breeze to clean. After cooking, a simple wipe-down of the exterior is usually all that's needed. This reduction in cleanup time makes the air fryer especially attractive for those who are short on time or don't enjoy spending long hours cleaning up after meals.

VERSATILITY

The versatility of the air fryer is another major benefit. It's not just for making fries or chicken wings. With the right accessories and a little creativity, the air fryer can tackle nearly any recipe you'd normally make in a conventional oven or stovetop.

You can use the air fryer to cook a variety of proteins, from crispy chicken breasts to juicy pork chops, and even fish fillets. It's also great for roasting vegetables, making them crisp-tender in no time. In addition to savory dishes, the air fryer can handle baking as well. From muffins to cakes to even cinnamon rolls, you can bake just about anything in your air fryer. The hot, circulating air creates an even cooking environment, ensuring that your baked goods come out golden and perfectly cooked.

The ability to cook multiple types of dishes also extends to snacks. You can make healthy versions of your favorite snacks, such as homemade granola, roasted nuts, or even air-fried tortilla chips. Whether you're cooking a quick snack, prepping dinner, or preparing a full meal, the air fryer provides the flexibility to do it all with ease.

TIPS FOR AIR FRYER BEGINNERS

If you're new to using an air fryer, it can take a little time to get the hang of it. But once you understand the basics, you'll find that it's an easy and efficient way to cook. Here are some essential tips to help you get the best results from your air fryer.

PREHEAT YOUR AIR FRYER

Preheating your air fryer is a crucial step that many beginners overlook. Just like an oven, preheating ensures that the appliance reaches the optimal cooking temperature before you add your food. This helps to achieve a crispy texture and even cooking. Simply set the temperature on the control panel and allow the air fryer to run for 3-5 minutes before adding your ingredients. Some models have a preheat feature, but if yours doesn't, it's worth getting into the habit of preheating manually.

DON'T OVERCROWD THE BASKET

For the best results, avoid overcrowding the basket. The air fryer works by circulating hot air around the food, so if the basket is too full, the air can't flow properly, leading to uneven cooking. If you're making a larger batch, cook the food in batches

WELCOME TO THE AIR FRYER REVOLUTION

or leave some space between each piece. This will ensure your food cooks evenly and crisps up as it should.

USE A LITTLE OIL

One of the great advantages of the air fryer is that you don't need much oil to get crispy, flavorful food. However, a light coating of oil can enhance crispiness and flavor. A spray bottle or a brush works best to apply a thin, even layer of oil to the food. Avoid soaking your food in oil, as it can cause excess grease to build up and make a mess.

SHAKE OR FLIP YOUR FOOD

To ensure even cooking, it's a good idea to shake or flip your food halfway through the cooking time. This is especially important for things like fries, chicken wings, or anything that might stick to the basket. Some air fryers even have an alert to remind you to shake the basket, but if yours doesn't, set a timer to help you remember.

CLEAN AND MAINTAIN REGULARLY

To keep your air fryer working at its best, cleaning is key. After each use, allow it to cool, then remove the basket and tray. Wash them with warm, soapy water or place them in the dishwasher if they're dishwasher-safe. For the main unit, wipe it down with a damp cloth. Be sure to regularly check the heating element for grease buildup, which can affect performance. A light cleaning after each use will help prevent long-term buildup.

CHAPTER 1

Air Fryer Cooking Chart

Beef

Item	Temp (°F)	Time (mins)	Item	Temp (°F)	Time (mins)
Beef Eye Round Roast (4 lbs.)	400 °F	45 to 55	Meatballs (1-inch)	370 °F	7
Burger Patty (4 oz.)	370 °F	16 to 20	Meatballs (3-inch)	380 °F	10
Filet Mignon (8 oz.)	400 °F	18	Ribeye, bone-in (1-inch, 8 oz)	400 °F	10 to 15
Flank Steak (1.5 lbs.)	400 °F	12	Sirloin steaks (1-inch, 12 oz)	400 °F	9 to 14
Flank Steak (2 lbs.)	400 °F	20 to 28			

Chicken

Item	Temp (°F)	Time (mins)	Item	Temp (°F)	Time (mins)
Breasts, bone in (1 ¼ lb.)	370 °F	25	Legs, bone-in (1 ¾ lb.)	380 °F	30
Breasts, boneless (4 oz)	380 °F	12	Thighs, boneless (1 ½ lb.)	380 °F	18 to 20
Drumsticks (2 ½ lb.)	370 °F	20	Wings (2 lb.)	400 °F	12
Game Hen (halved 2 lb.)	390 °F	20	Whole Chicken	360 °F	75
Thighs, bone-in (2 lb.)	380 °F	22	Tenders	360 °F	8 to 10

Pork & Lamb

Item	Temp (°F)	Time (mins)	Item	Temp (°F)	Time (mins)
Bacon (regular)	400 °F	5 to 7	Pork Tenderloin	370 °F	15
Bacon (thick cut)	400 °F	6 to 10	Sausages	380 °F	15
Pork Loin (2 lb.)	360 °F	55	Lamb Loin Chops (1-inch thick)	400 °F	8 to 12
Pork Chops, bone in (1-inch, 6.5 oz)	400 °F	12	Rack of Lamb (1.5 – 2 lb.)	380 °F	22

Fish & Seafood

Item	Temp (°F)	Time (mins)	Item	Temp (°F)	Time (mins)
Calamari (8 oz)	400 °F	4	Tuna Steak	400 °F	7 to 10
Fish Fillet (1-inch, 8 oz)	400 °F	10	Scallops	400 °F	5 to 7
Salmon, fillet (6 oz)	380 °F	12	Shrimp	400 °F	5
Swordfish steak	400 °F	10			

WELCOME TO THE AIR FRYER REVOLUTION

Air Fryer Cooking Chart

Vegetables					
INGREDIENT	AMOUNT	PREPARATION	OIL	TEMP	COOK TIME
Asparagus	2 bunches	Cut in half, trim stems	2 Tbsp	420°F	12-15 mins
Beets	1½ lbs	Peel, cut in ½-inch cubes	1 Tbsp	390°F	28-30 mins
Bell peppers (for roasting)	4 peppers	Cut in quarters, remove seeds	1 Tbsp	400°F	15-20 mins
Broccoli	1 large head	Cut in 1-2-inch florets	1 Tbsp	400°F	15-20 mins
Brussels sprouts	1 lb	Cut in half, remove stems	1 Tbsp	425°F	15-20 mins
Carrots	1 lb	Peel, cut in ¼-inch rounds	1 Tbsp	425°F	10-15 mins
Cauliflower	1 head	Cut in 1-2-inch florets	2 Tbsp	400°F	20-22 mins
Corn on the cob	7 ears	Whole ears, remove husks	1 Tbps	400°F	14-17 mins
Green beans	1 bag (12 oz)	Trim	1 Tbps	420°F	18-20 mins
Kale (for chips)	4 oz	Tear into pieces, remove stems	None	325°F	5-8 mins
Mushrooms	16 oz	Rinse, slice thinly	1 Tbps	390°F	25-30 mins
Potatoes, russet	1½ lbs	Cut in 1-inch wedges	1 Tbps	390°F	25-30 mins
Potatoes, russet	1 lb	Hand-cut fries, soak 30 mins in cold water, then pat dry	½ -3 Tbps	400°F	25-28 mins
Potatoes, sweet	1 lb	Hand-cut fries, soak 30 mins in cold water, then pat dry	1 Tbps	400°F	25-28 mins
Zucchini	1 lb	Cut in eighths lengthwise, then cut in half	1 Tbps	400°F	15-20 mins

CHAPTER 2: APPETIZERS AND SMALL BITES

APPETIZERS AND SMALL BITES

CHEESY BROCCOLI BITES

Prep time: 15 minutes | **Cook time:** 10 minutes | **Serves** 4

- 1 pound broccoli florets
- 1 teaspoon garlic powder
- 1 tablespoon dried onion flakes
- 1 teaspoon crushed red pepper flakes
- 2 tablespoons extra-virgin olive oil
- ½ cup grated Pecorino Romano cheese

1. In a large bowl, toss broccoli with olive oil and all seasonings until evenly coated.
2. Place the seasoned broccoli in the air fryer basket (no need to oil the basket).
3. Air fry at 370°F for 10 minutes, shaking the basket halfway through cooking.
4. Serve immediately while hot and crispy.

HAM AND CHEESE SPINACH DIP

Prep time: 8 minutes | **Cook time:** 7 minutes | **Makes** 1½ cups

- 1 (8 oz) package cream cheese, softened
- 1 cup shredded sharp cheddar cheese
- ½ cup mayonnaise
- ¼ cup grated Parmesan cheese
- 2 teaspoons minced garlic
- 1 tablespoon dried minced onion
- ½ cup diced ham
- ½ cup fresh baby spinach, roughly chopped

1. In a large bowl, combine softened cream cheese, cheddar, mayonnaise, Parmesan, garlic, and dried onion until well blended.
2. Gently fold in diced ham and chopped spinach.
3. Transfer mixture to a 6-7 inch oven-safe dish that fits in your air fryer basket.
4. Air fry at 350°F for 7-8 minutes until bubbly and heated through.
5. Serve hot with crackers, bread, or vegetables.

CHAPTER 2

ROASTED RANCH CHICKPEAS

Prep time: 5 minutes | **Cook time:** 15 minutes | **Makes** 1½ cups

- 1 (15 oz) can chickpeas
- 2 tablespoons olive oil, divided
- 1 (1 oz) packet ranch seasoning mix
- 1 teaspoon onion powder

1. Line air fryer basket with parchment paper.
2. Drain and rinse chickpeas, then pat very dry with paper towels.
3. In a medium bowl, toss chickpeas with 1 tablespoon olive oil, ranch seasoning, and onion powder.
4. Spread seasoned chickpeas in lined air fryer basket.
5. Air fry at 390°F for 15 minutes, shaking basket halfway through.
6. Transfer hot chickpeas to a bowl and toss with remaining tablespoon of olive oil.
7. Let cool slightly before serving. Store any leftovers in an airtight container.

CLASSIC FRENCH FRIES

Prep time: 5 minutes | **Cook time:** 25 minutes | **Serves** 2 to 3

- 2-3 russet potatoes
- 2-3 teaspoons vegetable oil
- Kosher salt, to taste

1. Peel potatoes and cut into ½-inch thick fries.
2. Bring large pot of salted water to boil. Blanch fries for 4 minutes.
3. Drain and rinse with cold water. Pat completely dry.
4. Preheat air fryer to 400°F.
5. Toss dried fries with oil.
6. Air fry at 400°F for 25 minutes, shaking basket several times.
7. Season with salt halfway through cooking.
8. Serve hot with ketchup, sriracha mayo, or parmesan-herb topping.

APPETIZERS AND SMALL BITES

SALMON NACHOS

Prep time: 10 minutes | **Cook time:** 9 to 12 minutes | **Serves** 6

- 36 baked corn tortilla chips (about 2 oz)
- 1 (5 oz) cooked salmon fillet, flaked
- ½ cup low-sodium black beans, rinsed and drained
- 1 red bell pepper, diced
- ½ cup carrots, shredded
- 1 jalapeño pepper, seeded and minced
- ⅓ cup reduced-fat Swiss cheese, shredded
- 1 medium tomato, diced

1. Preheat your air fryer to 375°F for about 3 minutes.
2. Place the tortilla chips in a single layer in a 6-inch round baking pan or tray that fits your air fryer basket.
3. Evenly spread the flaked salmon over the chips, followed by the black beans, diced bell pepper, shredded carrots, and minced jalapeño.
4. Sprinkle the shredded Swiss cheese evenly over the layered ingredients.
5. Place the pan in the air fryer and cook for 9-12 minutes, or until the cheese is melted and golden brown. Keep an eye on it towards the end to prevent burning.
6. Once the nachos are done, remove the pan from the air fryer and top with the diced tomatoes.
7. Serve immediately while hot for the best flavor and texture.

PUFF PASTRY-WRAPPED COCKTAIL SAUSAGES

Prep time: 15 minutes | **Cook time:** 8 minutes per batch | **Serves** 8

- 1 sheet frozen puff pastry (from a 17.25 oz package), thawed
- All-purpose flour, for dusting
- ¼ cup whole-grain Dijon mustard
- 32 cocktail smokies or mini hot dogs
- 1 large egg, beaten
- 2 tablespoons sesame seeds

1. Thaw puff pastry according to package directions.
2. Dust work surface lightly with flour. Roll pastry into an 18x12-inch rectangle.
3. Spread mustard evenly over pastry surface.
4. Cut rectangle lengthwise in half, then cut each half into 16 pieces (about 2x3 inches each).
5. Place one cocktail sausage on the short end of each pastry rectangle and roll up. Seal edges with water if needed.
6. Pierce each wrapped sausage once or twice with a fork.
7. Brush with beaten egg and sprinkle with sesame seeds.
8. Air fry in batches at 350°F for 8 minutes, or until golden brown.
9. Check at 6 minutes for desired brownness. Serve hot.

CHAPTER 2

CRISPY FRIED PICKLES

Prep time: 12 minutes | **Cook time:** 16 to 20 minutes | **Makes** 16 to 24 slices

- 3-4 large whole dill pickles
- 2 large eggs
- 2/3 cup panko breadcrumbs
- 1/3 cup grated Parmesan cheese
- ¼ teaspoon dried dill
- Cooking spray

1. Line the air fryer basket with parchment paper.
2. Slice pickles diagonally into ¼-inch thick slices.
3. Pat pickle slices thoroughly dry with paper towels.
4. In a shallow bowl, beat eggs until well combined.
5. In a separate shallow bowl, mix panko, Parmesan cheese, and dried dill.
6. Dip each pickle slice in egg, letting excess drip off, then coat thoroughly in panko mixture.
7. Arrange breaded pickles in a single layer in the lined air fryer basket.
8. Lightly coat with cooking spray and air fry at 375°F for 8-10 minutes until golden brown and crispy.
9. Work in batches as needed, serving each batch hot from the air fryer.

CRISPY KALE CHIPS WITH TEX-MEX DIP

Prep time: 10 minutes | **Cook time:** 18 minutes | **Serves** 8

For the dip:
- 1 cup plain Greek yogurt
- 1 tablespoon chili powder
- ⅓ cup chunky salsa, well drained

For the chips:
- 1 large bunch curly kale
- 1 tablespoon olive oil
- ¼ teaspoon coarse sea salt

1. Combine Greek yogurt, chili powder, and drained salsa in a bowl. Cover and refrigerate until ready to serve.
2. Remove stems and thick ribs from kale leaves. Tear leaves into 3-inch pieces.
3. Wash kale thoroughly and dry completely using a salad spinner or paper towels.
4. Toss dried kale pieces with olive oil in a large bowl, massaging oil into leaves.
5. Working in batches, arrange kale in a single layer in air fryer basket.
6. Air fry at 375°F for 5-6 minutes per batch, shaking basket halfway through.
7. Sprinkle each batch with sea salt while still hot.
8. Serve immediately with chilled Tex-Mex dip.

APPETIZERS AND SMALL BITES

ROASTED GRAPE AND BASIL DIP

Prep time: 10 minutes | **Cook time:** 8 to 12 minutes | **Serves** 6

- 2 cups red seedless grapes
- 1 tablespoon apple cider vinegar
- 1 tablespoon honey
- 1 cup low-fat Greek yogurt
- 2 tablespoons 2% milk
- 2 tablespoons fresh basil, finely chopped

1. Place grapes in air fryer basket. Drizzle with vinegar and honey, tossing to coat evenly.
2. Air fry at 375°F for 8-12 minutes until grapes are slightly shriveled but still soft.
3. In a medium bowl, whisk together yogurt and milk until smooth.
4. Fold in roasted grapes and chopped basil.
5. Serve immediately or refrigerate for 1-2 hours to chill.

SPICY SWEET POTATO FRIES

Prep time: 15 minutes | **Cook time:** 8 to 12 minutes | **Serves** 4

- 2 large sweet potatoes
- 1 teaspoon ground cumin
- 1 teaspoon paprika
- ½ teaspoon garlic powder
- ½ teaspoon cayenne pepper
- ⅛ teaspoon black pepper, freshly ground
- 1 cup lowfat Greek yogurt
- 2 teaspoons olive oil

1. Peel sweet potatoes and cut into 1/3-inch thick fries.
2. Soak fries in cold water while preparing spice mix.
3. Combine cumin, paprika, garlic powder, cayenne, and black pepper.
4. Mix half the spices with yogurt for dip; refrigerate.
5. Drain fries, pat completely dry with paper towels.
6. Toss fries with olive oil, then remaining spices.
7. Air fry at 400°F for 8-12 minutes until crispy and golden, shaking basket halfway through.
8. Serve hot with spiced yogurt dip.

CHAPTER 2

SHRIMP TOASTS

Prep time: 2 minutes | **Cook time:** 6 to 8 minutes | **Serves** 4 to 6

- ½ pound raw shrimp, peeled and deveined
- 1 large egg
- 2 scallions, chopped, plus more for garnish
- 2 teaspoons fresh ginger, grated
- 1 teaspoon soy sauce
- ½ teaspoon sesame oil
- 2 tablespoons fresh cilantro or parsley, chopped
- 1-2 teaspoons sriracha sauce
- 6 slices white sandwich bread, crusts removed
- ½ cup sesame seeds
- Sweet chili sauce, for serving

1. In food processor, combine shrimp, egg, scallions, ginger, soy sauce, sesame oil, herbs, and sriracha. Pulse to form chunky paste.
2. Spread shrimp mixture evenly on bread slices.
3. Press bread shrimp-side down in sesame seeds to coat.
4. Cut each slice into 4 triangles.
5. Preheat air fryer to 400°F.
6. Air fry in single layer for 6-8 minutes until sesame seeds are golden.
7. Garnish with sliced scallions and serve with sweet chili sauce.

ASIAN VEGETABLE POT STICKERS

Prep time: 12 minutes | **Cook time:** 11-18 minutes | **Makes** 12 pot stickers

- 1 cup red cabbage, shredded
- ¼ cup button mushrooms, finely chopped
- ¼ cup carrots, shredded
- 2 tablespoons onion, minced
- 2 cloves garlic, minced
- 2 teaspoons fresh ginger, grated
- 12 gyoza wrappers
- 2½ teaspoons vegetable oil, divided
- 2 tablespoons water, divided

1. In a 6-inch round pan, combine cabbage, mushrooms, carrots, onion, garlic, and ginger with 1 tablespoon water.
2. Air fry at 375°F for 3-6 minutes until vegetables are crisp-tender. Drain and cool slightly.
3. Place about 1 tablespoon filling in center of each wrapper.
4. Moisten wrapper edge with water, fold in half, and press to seal, creating pleats if desired.
5. Brush 6-inch pan with 1¼ teaspoons oil. Arrange 6 pot stickers seam-side up.
6. Air fry at 375°F for 5 minutes until bottoms are golden.
7. Add 1 tablespoon water and air fry 4-6 minutes more until heated through.
8. Repeat with remaining pot stickers, oil, and water.

CHAPTER 3: BREAKFAST FAVORITES

CHAPTER 3

MEATLESS BREAKFAST SAUSAGE

Prep time: 20 minutes | **Cook time:** 15 minutes | **Serves** 3

- 1 (15 oz) can white beans, drained and rinsed
- 1 medium yellow onion, chopped
- 2 cloves garlic, minced
- 2 tablespoons olive oil
- 1 teaspoon liquid smoke
- 2 tablespoons buckwheat flour

1. In a food processor, combine beans, onion, garlic, olive oil, liquid smoke, and flour.
2. Process until mixture is well combined but still has some texture.
3. Form mixture into 3 sausage-shaped patties.
4. Preheat air fryer to 390°F.
5. Place sausages in air fryer basket (no need to grease).
6. Cook for 15 minutes, flipping halfway through, until golden brown and heated through.

CHEESE OMELETTE

Prep time: 5 minutes | **Cook time:** 15 minutes | **Serves** 2

- 3 large eggs
- 1 large yellow onion, diced
- 2 tablespoons sharp cheddar cheese, shredded
- ½ teaspoon soy sauce
- Salt and pepper to taste
- Olive oil cooking spray

1. In a medium bowl whisk together eggs, soy sauce, pepper, and salt until well combined.
2. Spray with olive oil cooking spray in a small pan that will fit inside of your air fryer.
3. Add diced onions to the pan and spread them around evenly.
4. Air fry onions for 7 minutes until softened and lightly browned.
5. Pour the beaten egg mixture evenly over the cooked onions and sprinkle the top with shredded cheese.
6. Place back into the air fryer and cook for 6 minutes more until eggs are set.
7. Remove from the air fryer and serve omelet with toasted multi-grain bread.

BREAKFAST FAVORITES

SCRAMBLED PANCAKE HASH

Prep time: 7 minutes | **Cook time:** 9 minutes | **Serves** 7

- 1 large egg
- ¼ cup heavy cream
- 5 tablespoons butter, melted
- 1 cup coconut flour
- 1 teaspoon ground ginger
- 1 teaspoon salt
- 1 tablespoon apple cider vinegar
- 1 teaspoon baking soda

1. Combine the salt, baking soda, ground ginger and coconut flour in a mixing bowl.
2. In a separate bowl, crack the egg into it.
3. Add melted butter and heavy cream to the egg.
4. Mix well using a hand mixer until smooth.
5. Combine the liquid mixture and dry mixture and stir until completely smooth with no lumps.
6. Preheat your air fryer to 400°F.
7. Pour the pancake mixture evenly into the air fryer basket tray.
8. Cook the pancake hash for 4 minutes.
9. After this, scramble the pancake hash well with a spatula and continue to cook for another 5 minutes more.
10. When dish is cooked through and slightly crispy, transfer it to serving plates, and serve hot!

FRESH RASPBERRY SCONES

Prep time: 10 minutes | **Cook time:** 15 minutes | **Makes** 6 scones

- 1 cup all-purpose flour, plus extra for dusting
- 2½ tablespoons unsalted butter, cold and cubed
- 1 tablespoon granulated sugar
- 1½ teaspoons baking powder
- ¼ teaspoon salt
- ½ cup whole milk
- ½ cup fresh raspberries
- Olive oil spray
- Parchment paper

1. Line air fryer basket with parchment paper.
2. In a large mixing bowl, combine flour, cold butter cubes, sugar, baking powder, and salt.
3. Using clean hands, work ingredients together until mixture resembles coarse crumbs.
4. Make a well in center of flour mixture, then pour in milk.
5. Mix with hands until a thick dough forms.
6. Transfer dough to a well-floured work surface.
7. Gently fold in raspberries throughout the dough, being careful not to crush them.
8. Form dough into a ball and gently flatten into a disc.
9. Cut disc into 6 even wedges and transfer to lined air fryer basket.
10. Lightly spray scones with olive oil.
11. Bake for 5 minutes.
12. Carefully reposition scones in basket and bake 5 minutes more.
13. Flip scones over and bake final 5 minutes until golden brown. Serve warm.

CHAPTER 3

BREAKFAST CHICKEN STRIPS

Prep time: 5 minutes | **Cook time:** 12 minutes | **Serves** 4

- 1 teaspoon paprika
- 1 tablespoon heavy cream
- 1 pound chicken fillet
- ½ teaspoon salt
- ½ teaspoon black pepper

1. Cut the chicken fillet into even-sized strips.
2. Sprinkle the chicken fillets evenly with salt and pepper on both sides.
3. Preheat the air fryer to 365°F.
4. Place the butter in the air fryer basket tray and add the seasoned chicken strips.
5. Cook the chicken strips for 6 minutes.
6. Turn the chicken strips to the other side and cook them for an additional 5 minutes.
7. After strips are cooked, drizzle them with cream and sprinkle with paprika, then transfer them to serving plates. Serve while warm.

HERBED BREAKFAST EGGS

Prep time: 5 minutes | **Cook time:** 17 minutes | **Serves** 2

- 4 large eggs
- 1 teaspoon dried oregano
- 1 teaspoon dried parsley
- ½ teaspoon sea salt
- 1 tablespoon fresh chives, chopped
- 1 tablespoon heavy cream
- 1 teaspoon paprika

1. Place the eggs in the air fryer basket and cook them for 17 minutes at 320°F.
2. Meanwhile, combine the dried parsley, oregano, cream, and salt in a shallow bowl.
3. Chop the chives and add them to the cream mixture.
4. When the eggs are cooked, place them in a bowl of cold water and allow them to chill completely.
5. After this, carefully peel the eggs and cut them into halves lengthwise.
6. Remove the egg yolks and add the yolks to cream mixture and mash to blend well with a fork.
7. Then fill the egg white halves evenly with the cream-egg yolk mixture. Serve immediately.

BREAKFAST FAVORITES

ITALIAN BREAKFAST FRITTATA

Prep time: 5 minutes | **Cook time:** 10 minutes | **Serves** 2

- 4 cherry tomatoes, sliced into halves
- ½ pound Italian sausage, sliced
- ½ teaspoon Italian seasoning
- 3 large eggs
- 2 ounces Parmesan cheese, freshly shredded
- 1 tablespoon fresh parsley, chopped
- Salt and pepper to taste

1. Preheat your air fryer to 360°F.
2. Put the sliced sausage and cherry tomatoes into an air fryer-safe baking dish and cook for 5 minutes.
3. Crack eggs into a small bowl, add chopped parsley, Italian seasoning and mix well by whisking until combined.
4. Pour the egg mixture evenly over the sausage and cherry tomatoes and place back into air fryer to cook for an additional 5 minutes. Serve warm.

BREAKFAST TUNA & BACON

Prep time: 8 minutes | **Cook time:** 10 minutes | **Serves** 4

- 6 ounces bacon, cut into pieces
- 1 teaspoon butter
- 4 ounces Parmesan cheese, freshly shredded
- 1 teaspoon heavy cream
- 6 ounces canned tuna, drained
- ½ teaspoon black pepper, freshly ground
- ¼ teaspoon ground turmeric
- ¼ teaspoon sea salt

1. Divide bacon pieces evenly inside four oven-safe ramekins.
2. Add a small amount of butter (about ¼ teaspoon) in each ramekin.
3. Mix the sea salt, turmeric, and black pepper in a small bowl.
4. In a separate bowl, flake the tuna and mix with the spice blend until well combined.
5. Divide the seasoned tuna mixture evenly into each ramekin on top of bacon.
6. Drizzle ¼ teaspoon cream and sprinkle shredded cheese over tuna in each ramekin.
7. Preheat your air fryer to 360°F.
8. Place the ramekins into the air fryer basket and cook for 10 minutes.
9. When done, the top should be light golden brown and slightly crispy. Serve hot!

CHAPTER 3

GOURMET GRILLED CHEESE

Prep time: 5 minutes | **Cook time:** 8 minutes | **Serves** 2

- 2 tablespoons mayonnaise
- 4 thick slices sourdough bread
- 4 thick slices Brie cheese
- 8 slices hot capicola
- Air fryer parchment paper (optional)

1. Spread mayonnaise evenly on one side of each bread slice.
2. Place 2 bread slices in air fryer basket, mayonnaise-side down.
3. Layer Brie slices and capicola evenly on bread in basket.
4. Top with remaining bread slices, mayonnaise-side up.
5. Set air fryer to 350°F and cook 8 minutes until cheese melts and bread is golden brown.
6. Serve immediately while hot and crispy.

CHEESY PUFF PASTRY EGG TARTS

Prep time: 10 minutes | **Cook time:** 17 to 20 minutes | **Makes** 2 tarts

- ⅓ sheet frozen puff pastry, thawed
- ½ cup sharp cheddar cheese, shredded
- 2 large eggs
- ¼ teaspoon kosher salt
- 1 teaspoon fresh parsley, minced (optional garnish)
- Parchment paper

1. Place puff pastry on parchment paper and cut into two equal squares.
2. Transfer both pastry squares (on parchment) to air fryer basket.
3. Bake at 375°F for 10 minutes until golden brown.
4. Carefully press down center of each pastry with back of metal spoon to create wells.
5. Divide shredded cheese equally between pastries.
6. Crack one egg onto cheese layer in each pastry.
7. Sprinkle ⅛ teaspoon salt over each egg.
8. Bake 7-10 minutes more until eggs are set to desired doneness.
9. If using, garnish with fresh parsley before serving.

BREAKFAST FAVORITES

VEGGIE & CHEESE EGG CUPS

Prep time: 10 minutes | **Cook time:** 19 minutes | Serves 2

- 2 large eggs
- ½ cup mixed vegetables, diced (onions, bell peppers, mushrooms, tomatoes)
- ½ cup sharp cheddar cheese, shredded, divided
- 2 tablespoons half-and-half
- 1 tablespoon fresh cilantro (or herb of choice), chopped
- Kosher salt and black pepper to taste
- Vegetable oil for greasing

1. Lightly grease two 6-ounce ramekins with vegetable oil.
2. In medium bowl, whisk together eggs, diced vegetables, ¼ cup cheese, half-and-half, cilantro, salt, and pepper.
3. Divide mixture evenly between prepared ramekins.
4. Place ramekins in air fryer basket.
5. Cook at 300°F for 15 minutes.
6. Top each cup with remaining cheese (divided equally).
7. Increase temperature to 400°F and cook 4 minutes until cheese melts and browns lightly.
8. Serve hot, or refrigerate in airtight container up to one week.

PECAN ROLLED OAT GRANOLA

Prep time: 5 minutes | **Cook time:** 5 minutes | Serves 6

- 1½ cups old-fashioned rolled oats
- ½ cup pecans, roughly chopped
- ¼ teaspoon salt
- ½ cup raisins
- ½ cup raw sunflower seeds
- 2 tablespoons butter, melted
- 2 teaspoons liquid stevia
- Cooking spray

1. In a large mixing bowl, combine oats, seeds, pecans and a dash of salt and stir well to mix.
2. In a small bowl mix melted butter with stevia then add to oat mixture, stirring to coat evenly.
3. Spray the inside of an air fryer-safe baking pan with cooking spray and add in the oat mixture.
4. Set your air fryer to 350°F and cook for 5 minutes.
5. Stir mixture halfway through cooking time for even browning.
6. Remove from air fryer and pour into a large bowl to cool completely.
7. Add the sunflower seeds and raisins and stir to combine.
8. Eat immediately or store in an airtight container for up to 2 weeks.

CHAPTER 4: POULTRY DISHES

POULTRY DISHES

EASY CHICKEN NUGGETS

Prep time: 15 minutes | **Cook time:** 12 minutes | **Serves** 4

- 1 large egg, whisked
- ¼ cup all-purpose flour
- 1 cup seasoned breadcrumbs
- 1 tablespoon olive oil
- Sea salt and ground black pepper, to taste
- 1 ½ pounds boneless, skinless chicken breasts, cut into bite-sized pieces

1. In a shallow bowl, whisk together the egg and flour. In another bowl, combine the breadcrumbs, olive oil, salt, and black pepper.
2. Dip the chicken pieces into the egg mixture, then roll them in the breadcrumb mixture until fully coated.
3. Preheat the Air Fryer to 380°F. Arrange the chicken nuggets in the Air Fryer basket and cook for 12 minutes, flipping halfway through the cooking time.
4. Serve hot with your favorite dipping sauce. Enjoy!

BBQ TURKEY BREASTS

Prep time: 25 minutes | **Cook time:** 1 hour | **Serves** 5

- 2 tablespoons olive oil
- Sea salt and freshly cracked black pepper, to taste
- 1 tablespoon Dijon mustard
- 1 tablespoon hot sauce
- 1 teaspoon smoked paprika
- 1 teaspoon dried basil
- 1 teaspoon dried thyme
- 2 pounds turkey breast, bone-in

1. In a mixing bowl, thoroughly combine the olive oil, salt, black pepper, mustard, hot sauce, paprika, basil, and thyme.
2. Rub the mixture evenly over the turkey breasts.
3. Preheat the Air Fryer to 350°F. Cook the turkey breasts for 1 hour, turning them over every 20 minutes.
4. Let the turkey rest for 5 minutes before slicing and serving.
5. Enjoy your flavorful BBQ turkey!

CHAPTER 4

CHICKEN CORDON BLEU

Prep time: 15 minutes | **Cook time:** 25 minutes | **Serves** 4

- 2 (8-ounce) boneless, skinless chicken breasts
- 8 thin slices deli ham
- 4 slices Swiss cheese
- ½ teaspoon black pepper
- 1 large egg
- ¾ cup panko breadcrumbs or crushed pork rinds
- Vegetable oil spray

1. Cut each chicken breast in half horizontally to create 4 thin cutlets. Place 2 slices of ham and 1 slice of Swiss cheese on each piece of chicken. Sprinkle with pepper.
2. Roll up each piece of chicken and secure with a toothpick.
3. In a shallow bowl, beat the egg. Place the panko breadcrumbs (or crushed pork rinds) on a plate. Dip each chicken roll in the egg, then coat with the breadcrumbs. Spray all sides generously with vegetable oil spray.
4. Preheat the Air Fryer to 350°F.
5. Place the chicken rolls in the Air Fryer basket and cook for 25 minutes, turning the chicken halfway through and spraying with oil spray again.
6. Use a meat thermometer to ensure the chicken has reached an internal temperature of 165°F.
7. Serve hot and enjoy!

HAM AND CHEESE STUFFED CHICKEN

Prep time: 25 minutes | **Cook time:** 22 minutes | **Serves** 4

- 1 pound boneless, skinless chicken breasts, cut into 4 slices
- 4 ounces goat cheese, crumbled
- 4 ounces ham, chopped
- 1 large egg
- ¼ cup all-purpose flour
- ¼ cup grated Parmesan cheese
- ½ teaspoon onion powder
- ½ teaspoon garlic powder

1. Use a meat mallet to flatten the chicken breasts to an even thickness.
2. Stuff each chicken breast with goat cheese and ham. Roll up the chicken and secure with toothpicks.
3. In a shallow bowl, combine the egg, flour, Parmesan cheese, onion powder, and garlic powder. Dip the chicken rolls into the egg mixture, ensuring they are fully coated.
4. Preheat the Air Fryer to 400°F. Arrange the stuffed chicken in the Air Fryer basket and cook for about 22 minutes, turning halfway through the cooking time.
5. Let the chicken rest for a few minutes before serving. Enjoy!

POULTRY DISHES

TURKEY AND AVOCADO SLIDERS

Prep time: 25 minutes | **Cook time:** 17 minutes | **Serves** 4

- 1 pound ground turkey
- 1 tablespoon olive oil
- 1 avocado, peeled, pitted, and chopped
- 2 garlic cloves, minced
- ½ cup breadcrumbs
- Kosher salt and ground black pepper, to taste
- 8 small slider rolls

1. In a mixing bowl, combine the ground turkey, olive oil, avocado, garlic, breadcrumbs, salt, and black pepper. Mix until well combined. Form the mixture into 8 small patties.
2. Preheat the Air Fryer to 380°F. Cook the patties for about 17 minutes, turning halfway through the cooking time, until fully cooked.
3. Serve the turkey patties on the prepared rolls. Enjoy!

OLD BAY CRISPY CHICKEN WINGS

Prep time: 5 minutes | **Cook time:** 40 minutes | **Serves** 4

- 3 pounds bone-in chicken wings
- ¾ cup almond flour
- 1 tablespoon Old Bay seasoning
- 2 fresh lemons, juiced
- 4 tablespoons butter

1. In a bowl, mix the Old Bay seasoning and almond flour.
2. Add the chicken wings and toss well to coat.
3. Preheat your Air Fryer to 375°F.
4. Shake off any excess flour and transfer the wings to the Air Fryer basket.
5. Work in batches to avoid overcrowding the basket.
6. Cook for 40 minutes, shaking the basket occasionally.
7. Meanwhile, melt the butter in a saucepan over low heat.
8. Stir in the lemon juice and mix to combine.
9. Serve the wings hot, drizzling the lemon butter over them. Enjoy!

CHAPTER 4

TURKEY SAUSAGE PATTIES

Prep time: 5 minutes | **Cook time:** 4 minutes | **Serves** 6

- 1 teaspoon olive oil
- 1 small onion, diced
- 1 large garlic clove, chopped
- Salt and pepper, to taste
- 1 tablespoon vinegar
- 1 tablespoon chopped chives
- ¾ teaspoon paprika
- Pinch of nutmeg
- 1 lb. lean ground turkey
- 1 teaspoon fennel seeds

1. Preheat your Air Fryer to 375°F.
2. Add half of the olive oil to the Air Fryer, along with the onion and garlic. Air fry for 1 minute. Add the fennel seeds and transfer the mixture to a plate.
3. In a mixing bowl, combine the paprika, ground turkey, nutmeg, chives, vinegar, salt, pepper, and the onion mixture. Mix well and form into patties.
4. Add the remaining oil to the Air Fryer basket. Place the patties in the basket and air fry for 3 minutes.
5. Serve on buns and enjoy!

TERIYAKI CHICKEN KEBABS

Prep time: 10 minutes | **Cook time:** 9 to 10 minutes | **Makes** 4 kebabs

For the glaze:
- ⅓ cup honey
- ⅓ cup teriyaki sauce
- ½ teaspoon salt
- ½ teaspoon ground black pepper

For the kebabs:
- 1 bell pepper, any color, chopped
- 6 small cremini mushrooms, halved
- ½ cup pineapple chunks
- 4 boneless, skinless chicken thighs, cut into cubes or strips
- Olive oil spray
- ¼ teaspoon sesame seeds

1. Place the chopped bell pepper, mushrooms, and pineapple in separate bowls.
2. Slice the chicken thighs into cubes or strips.
3. Assemble the kebabs by threading the vegetables and chicken onto metal skewers, alternating between the ingredients.
4. Lightly spray the kebabs with olive oil and place them in the Air Fryer basket.
5. Preheat the Air Fryer to 400°F. Cook the kebabs for 8 minutes or until the chicken reaches an internal temperature of 180°F and the juices run clear.
6. Brush the teriyaki glaze over the cooked kebabs and cook for an additional 1-2 minutes, until the glaze is sticky and caramelized.
7. Sprinkle with sesame seeds before serving. Enjoy!

POULTRY DISHES

CHICKEN MEATBALLS

Prep time: 15 minutes | **Cook time:** 15 minutes | **Serves** 10

- 2 chicken breasts
- 1 tablespoon mustard powder
- Salt and pepper, to taste
- 1 onion, diced
- 2 tablespoons honey
- 3 tablespoons soy sauce
- 1 teaspoon chili powder
- 1 tablespoon thyme
- 1 tablespoon basil
- 1 tablespoon cumin

1. Cut the chicken breasts into chunks, ensuring they're small enough to process easily.
2. Add the chicken chunks to a food processor and pulse until finely minced, scraping down the sides as needed.
3. Add the mustard powder, salt, pepper, diced onion, honey, soy sauce, chili powder, thyme, basil, and cumin to the food processor. Pulse a few times until all the ingredients are well combined and the mixture is smooth.
4. With wet hands or a spoon, form the chicken mixture into small meatballs, about 1 to 1.5 inches in diameter.
5. Preheat your air fryer to 350°F for about 3 minutes.
6. Place the meatballs in the air fryer basket in a single layer, making sure they are not touching for even cooking. Cook for 15 minutes, flipping halfway through, until they're golden brown and fully cooked through (the internal temperature should reach 165°F).
7. Once cooked, remove the meatballs from the air fryer. Serve hot with your favorite dipping sauce or side dish.

PARMESAN CRUSTED CHICKEN FILLET

Prep time: 5 minutes | **Cook time:** 6 minutes | **Serves** 3

- 8 chicken fillets
- 1 egg, beaten
- 1 ounce garlic powder
- ½ cup grated Parmesan cheese
- 1 cup breadcrumbs
- 1 teaspoon Italian seasoning
- 1 ounce salted butter, melted

1. In a bowl, whisk together the egg, melted butter, garlic powder, and Italian seasoning.
2. Marinate the chicken fillets in the egg mixture for a few minutes.
3. In a separate bowl, combine the breadcrumbs and Parmesan cheese. Coat the chicken fillets with the breadcrumb mixture.
4. Set the coated fillets aside for 10 minutes.
5. Preheat the Air Fryer to 390°F for 3 minutes.
6. Line the Air Fryer basket with aluminum foil.
7. Place 4 pieces of chicken on the foil and cook for 6 minutes, without flipping.
8. Repeat the procedure for the remaining chicken fillets.
9. Serve hot and enjoy!

CHAPTER 4

HOT & SPICY BUFFALO WINGS

Prep time: 5 minutes | **Cook time:** 26 minutes | **Serves** 4

- 2 pounds chicken wings
- 6 tablespoons melted butter, divided
- Salt, to taste
- ½ cup hot & spicy sauce, divided

1. In a bowl, mix ¼ cup of hot sauce and 3 tablespoons of melted butter.
2. Coat the chicken wings with the sauce mixture and marinate for 2 hours in the fridge.
3. Preheat your Air Fryer to 400°F.
4. Split the wings into 2 batches.
5. Place the first batch of wings in the Air Fryer and cook for 12 minutes, shaking the basket halfway through.
6. Repeat with the second batch.
7. After both batches are done, cook the wings for an additional 2 minutes in the Air Fryer.
8. For the finishing sauce, mix the remaining 3 tablespoons of butter with the remaining ¼ cup of hot sauce.
9. Dip the cooked wings in the sauce, serve, and enjoy!

AUTHENTIC CHICKEN FAJITAS

Prep time: 35 minutes | **Cook time:** 15 minutes | **Serves** 4

- 1 pound boneless, skinless chicken thighs, cut into pieces
- 2 tablespoons canola oil
- 1 red bell pepper, sliced
- 1 yellow bell pepper, sliced
- 1 jalapeño pepper, sliced
- 1 onion, sliced
- ½ teaspoon onion powder
- ½ teaspoon garlic powder
- Sea salt and ground black pepper, to taste

1. Pat the chicken dry with paper towels. Toss the chicken pieces with 1 tablespoon of the canola oil.
2. Preheat the Air Fryer to 380°F. Cook the chicken for 15 minutes, shaking the basket halfway through the cooking time.
3. Add the bell peppers, jalapeño, onion, onion powder, garlic powder, salt, and black pepper to the Air Fryer basket. Increase the temperature to 400°F. Cook for an additional 15 minutes, or until the vegetables are tender and the chicken is fully cooked.
4. Serve immediately and enjoy!

CHAPTER 5: MEAT RECIPES

CHAPTER 5

ROSEMARY RIBEYE STEAK

Prep time: 20 minutes | **Cook time:** 15 minutes | **Serves** 4

- 1 pound ribeye steak, bone-in
- 2 tablespoons butter, room temperature
- 2 garlic cloves, minced
- Sea salt and ground black pepper, to taste
- 2 rosemary sprigs, leaves picked, chopped

1. Pat the ribeye steak dry with paper towels to remove any moisture. This will help it sear better in the air fryer.
2. In a small bowl, mix together the room temperature butter, minced garlic, sea salt, black pepper, and chopped rosemary leaves. Stir until the ingredients are well combined.
3. Rub the rosemary butter mixture evenly over both sides of the ribeye steak, ensuring it's fully coated.
4. Set your air fryer to 400°F and preheat for about 3 minutes.
5. Place the ribeye steak in the air fryer basket, making sure it's not touching the sides. Cook for 15 minutes, flipping halfway through the cooking time, for a medium-rare steak. Adjust the time if you prefer it more well-done. (For medium, cook for about 16-17 minutes, and for well-done, cook for 18-20 minutes.)
6. Once the steak is cooked to your desired doneness, remove it from the air fryer and let it rest for 5 minutes. This helps the juices redistribute and keeps the steak tender.
7. Slice the ribeye against the grain and serve immediately while hot.

BEEF SHOULDER WITH ONION

Prep time: 55 minutes | **Cook time:** 45 minutes | **Serves** 4

- 1½ pounds beef shoulder
- Sea salt and ground black pepper, to taste
- 1 teaspoon cayenne pepper
- ½ teaspoon ground cumin
- 2 tablespoons olive oil
- 2 cloves garlic, minced
- 1 teaspoon Dijon mustard
- 1 onion, sliced

1. Trim any excess fat from the beef shoulder, then cut it into a few smaller pieces if needed to fit into your air fryer. Pat the beef dry with paper towels to help the seasoning stick.
2. In a bowl, combine the sea salt, black pepper, cayenne pepper, ground cumin, minced garlic, Dijon mustard, and olive oil. Rub this mixture evenly over the beef shoulder, making sure to coat all sides well. Let the beef sit for 10 minutes to marinate.
3. Set your air fryer to 390°F and preheat for about 3 minutes.
4. Lightly oil the air fryer basket, then place the seasoned beef shoulder inside. Cook for 45 minutes, turning the beef halfway through the cooking time to ensure even cooking.
5. After the first 45 minutes, open the air fryer and carefully add the sliced onion around the beef. Drizzle a little olive oil over the onions if desired.
6. Continue to cook for an additional 10 minutes, or until the beef is cooked through and the onions are tender and caramelized.
7. Remove the beef from the air fryer and let it rest for 5 minutes before slicing. This helps retain the juices for a tender result.
8. Slice the beef against the grain and serve with the caramelized onions on top. Enjoy!

MEAT RECIPES

TENDERLOIN STEAKS WITH MUSHROOMS

Prep time: 20 minutes | **Cook time:** 15 minutes | **Serves** 4

- 1½ pounds tenderloin steaks
- 2 tablespoons butter, melted
- 1 teaspoon garlic powder
- ½ teaspoon mustard powder
- 1 teaspoon cayenne pepper
- Sea salt and ground black pepper, to taste
- ½ pound cremini mushrooms, sliced

1. Toss the beef with 1 tablespoon of the melted butter and the spices.
2. Place the beef in the Air Fryer cooking basket.
3. Cook the beef at 400°F for 10 minutes, turning it over halfway through the cooking time.
4. Add the mushrooms and the remaining 1 tablespoon of butter. Continue to cook for an additional 5 minutes.
5. Serve warm and enjoy!

HERB BUTTER STEAK

Prep time: 15 minutes | **Cook time:** 12 minutes | **Serves** 5

- 2 pounds ribeye steaks, bone-in
- Kosher salt and freshly ground black pepper, to taste
- 3 tablespoons butter
- 1 tablespoon fresh basil, minced
- 1 tablespoon fresh parsley, minced
- 2 tablespoons fresh scallions, minced
- 2 cloves garlic, minced

1. Toss the steaks with the salt and black pepper.
2. Place the steaks in a lightly oiled Air Fryer cooking basket.
3. Cook the steaks at 400°F for 12 minutes, turning them over halfway through the cooking time.
4. In the meantime, mix the butter with the basil, parsley, scallions, and garlic. Place the butter mixture in the refrigerator until well-chilled.
5. Serve the warm steak with the chilled herb butter and enjoy!

CHAPTER 5

BBQ PORK CHOPS

Prep time: 5 minutes | **Cook time:** 10 minutes | **Serves** 6

- 6 pork loin chops
- Pepper, to taste
- 1 garlic clove, minced
- ¼ teaspoon ground ginger
- 1 teaspoon balsamic vinegar
- 2 tablespoons soy sauce
- 2 tablespoons honey

1. Preheat the air fryer to 350°F for 5 minutes.
2. Season the pork chops with pepper.
3. In a mixing bowl, combine soy sauce, honey, ground ginger, garlic, and balsamic vinegar. Mix well.
4. Add the seasoned pork chops to the bowl and coat them well.
5. Place the marinated pork chops in the fridge for 2 hours.
6. Place the marinated pork chops in the Air Fryer basket and cook for 10 minutes (5 minutes per side).

BEEF ROLL-UP

Prep time: 5 minutes | **Cook time:** 14 minutes | **Serves** 4

- 2 pounds beef flank steak
- Salt and pepper, to taste
- ¾ cup baby spinach, fresh
- 3 ounces roasted red bell peppers
- 6 slices provolone cheese
- 3 tablespoons pesto

1. Open the steak and spread the pesto evenly over the meat.
2. Layer the cheese, roasted red peppers, and spinach ¾ of the way down the steak.
3. Roll up the steak and secure it with toothpicks.
4. Season with salt and pepper.
5. Preheat the air fryer to 400°F.
6. Place the roll-ups in the Air Fryer basket and cook for 14 minutes.
7. Halfway through the cook time, rotate the meat.
8. After cooking, let the meat rest for 10 minutes before cutting and serving.

MEAT RECIPES

BREADED PORK CUTLETS

Prep time: 20 minutes | **Cook time:** 15 minutes | **Serves** 4

- 1½ pounds pork cutlets
- Seasoned salt and ground black pepper, to taste
- 1 cup tortilla chips, crushed
- ½ teaspoon cayenne pepper
- 2 tablespoons olive oil

1. Toss the pork cutlets with the crushed tortilla chips, cayenne pepper, and olive oil.
2. Place the cutlets in a lightly oiled Air Fryer cooking basket.
3. Cook the pork cutlets at 400°F for 15 minutes, turning them over halfway through the cooking time.
4. Serve hot and enjoy!

STICKY BACON WITH CAULIFLOWER

Prep time: 15 minutes | **Cook time:** 12 minutes | **Serves** 4

- 1 pound bacon, cut into thick slices
- 1 pound cauliflower, cut into florets
- 1 tablespoon maple syrup
- 1 teaspoon paprika
- Kosher salt and ground black pepper, to taste
- 2 cloves garlic, minced

1. Cut the bacon into thick slices, about 2-3 inches wide. This will help it cook evenly and crisp up in the air fryer.
2. Cut the cauliflower into bite-sized florets, ensuring they're relatively uniform in size for even cooking.
3. In a large bowl, toss the cauliflower florets with maple syrup, paprika, kosher salt, black pepper, and minced garlic. Add the cut bacon pieces to the bowl and toss everything together until the bacon and cauliflower are evenly coated.
4. Preheat your air fryer to 400°F for about 3 minutes.
5. Place the bacon and cauliflower mixture into the air fryer basket in a single layer. If needed, you can cook in two batches. Cook at 400°F for about 12 minutes, turning halfway through the cooking time to ensure even crisping and caramelization.
6. After 12 minutes, check to see if the bacon is crispy and the cauliflower is tender. If you prefer your bacon extra crispy, cook for another 2-3 minutes.
7. Once done, remove the bacon and cauliflower from the air fryer. Serve immediately while hot and enjoy the sticky, savory goodness!

CHAPTER 5

CLASSIC BEEF POT ROAST

Prep time: 10 minutes | **Cook time:** 1 hour | **Serves** 4

- 1 lb. chuck roast
- 4 spring onions
- 2 cinnamon sticks
- 2 tablespoons ginger garlic paste
- 2 tablespoons olive oil
- 1 teaspoon paprika
- 2 cardamoms
- 1 cup water
- ½ cup fresh coriander, chopped
- Salt and pepper, to taste
- 1 bay leaf

1. Preheat your air fryer to 400°F.
2. Cut the chuck roast into medium-sized chunks.
3. In a large bowl, add beef, onions, ginger garlic paste, salt, pepper, bay leaf, coriander, cardamoms, paprika, and water.
4. Mix well and marinate for 1 hour.
5. Add everything to a casserole dish and roast in the air fryer for 1 hour.
6. Remove the bay leaf and serve hot!

JUICY SEASONED PORK TENDERLOIN

Prep time: 25 minutes | **Cook time:** 50 minutes | **Makes** 15 medallion slices

- 1 (3-pound) pork tenderloin
- Olive oil spray
- 2 teaspoons granulated garlic, divided
- 1 teaspoon onion powder, divided
- 1 teaspoon seasoning salt, divided
- ½ teaspoon ground black pepper, divided

1. Remove the tenderloin from the refrigerator and bring it to room temperature (about 20 minutes). Slice the tenderloin in half (don't cut lengthwise) to make 2 shorter pieces.
2. Use paper towels to dry any moisture from the tenderloin pieces.
3. Spray the tenderloin with olive oil and sprinkle on half of the granulated garlic, onion powder, seasoning salt, and black pepper.
4. Place the tenderloin pieces in the Air Fryer basket and bake for 25 minutes.
5. Flip the tenderloin pieces, spray again with olive oil, and sprinkle with the remaining seasonings.
6. Return the tenderloin to the Air Fryer and bake for an additional 15 minutes, or until the internal temperature reaches 145°F to 150°F, and the meat is pale with mostly clear juices.
7. Remove the tenderloin pieces from the Air Fryer and allow them to rest for 10 minutes before slicing and serving.

CHAPTER 6: FISH AND SEAFOOD CREATIONS

CHAPTER 6

GREEK FISH PITA

Prep time: 15 minutes | **Cook time:** 35 minutes | **Serves** 4

- 1 pound monkfish fillets
- 1 tablespoon olive oil
- Sea salt and ground black pepper, to taste
- 1 teaspoon cayenne pepper
- 4 tablespoons coleslaw
- 1 avocado, pitted, peeled, and diced
- 1 tablespoon fresh parsley, chopped
- 4 (6½-inch) Greek pitas, warmed

1. Toss the fish fillets with olive oil and season with salt, pepper, and cayenne pepper. Place the fillets in a lightly oiled Air Fryer basket.
2. Cook the fish fillets at 400°F for about 14 minutes, turning them halfway through the cooking time.
3. Assemble the pitas with the cooked fish, coleslaw, avocado, and parsley. Serve warm.
4. Enjoy!

FRIED FISH FINGERS

Prep time: 10 minutes | **Cook time:** 10 minutes | **Serves** 4

- 2 eggs
- ½ cup all-purpose flour
- Sea salt and ground black pepper, to taste
- ½ teaspoon onion powder
- ¼ teaspoon garlic powder
- ¼ cup plain breadcrumbs
- 1½ tablespoons olive oil
- 1 pound cod fish fillets, sliced into pieces

1. In a mixing bowl, combine the eggs, flour, and spices.
2. In a separate bowl, combine the breadcrumbs and olive oil.
3. Dip the fish pieces into the flour mixture to coat, then roll them in the breadcrumb mixture until fully coated.
4. Cook the fish fingers at 400°F for 10 minutes, turning them halfway through the cooking time.
5. Serve hot and enjoy!

FISH AND SEAFOOD CREATIONS

CRISPY SALMON STICKS

Prep time: 15 minutes | **Cook time:** 10 minutes | **Serves** 4

- 1 egg, beaten
- ½ cup all-purpose flour
- Sea salt and ground black pepper, to taste
- 1 teaspoon hot paprika
- ½ cup seasoned breadcrumbs
- 1 tablespoon olive oil
- 1 pound salmon strips

1. In a mixing bowl, combine the egg, flour, and spices.
2. In a separate bowl, combine the breadcrumbs and olive oil.
3. Dip the salmon strips into the flour mixture, then coat them with the breadcrumb mixture.
4. Cook the salmon sticks at 400°F for 10 minutes, turning halfway through.
5. Serve hot and enjoy!

CLASSIC FISH BURGERS

Prep time: 15 minutes | **Cook time:** 14 minutes | **Serves** 4

- 1 pound halibut, chopped
- 2 garlic cloves, crushed
- 4 tablespoons scallions, chopped
- Sea salt and ground black pepper, to taste
- 1 teaspoon smoked paprika
- Pinch of grated nutmeg
- 1 tablespoon olive oil
- 4 hamburger buns

1. Mix the halibut, garlic, scallions, salt, pepper, paprika, nutmeg, and olive oil in a bowl. Shape the mixture into four patties.
2. Place the patties in a lightly oiled Air Fryer basket.
3. Cook the fish patties at 400°F for about 14 minutes, turning halfway through the cooking time.
4. Serve the patties on hamburger buns and enjoy!

CHAPTER 6

CRUNCHY FISH TACO

Prep time: 5 minutes | **Cook time:** 13 minutes | **Serves** 4

- 12-ounce cod fillet
- Salt and black pepper, to taste
- 1 cup tempura batter
- 1 cup breadcrumbs
- ½ cup guacamole
- 6 flour tortillas
- 2 tablespoons cilantro, freshly chopped
- ½ cup salsa
- 1 lemon, juiced

1. Cut the cod fillets lengthwise into 2-inch pieces and season with salt and pepper.
2. Dip each cod strip into tempura batter, then into breadcrumbs.
3. Preheat your air fryer to 340°F and cook the cod for 13 minutes.
4. Spread guacamole on each tortilla.
5. Place the cooked cod on the tortillas and top with chopped cilantro and salsa.
6. Squeeze lemon juice over the tacos, fold, and serve.

TUNA WRAPS

Prep time: 10 minutes | **Cook time:** 4 to 7 minutes | **Serves** 4

- 1 pound fresh tuna steak, cut into 1-inch cubes
- 1 tablespoon grated fresh ginger
- 2 garlic cloves, minced
- ½ teaspoon toasted sesame oil
- 4 low-sodium whole-wheat tortillas
- ¼ cup low-fat mayonnaise
- 2 cups shredded romaine lettuce
- 1 red bell pepper, thinly sliced

1. In a medium bowl, mix the tuna, ginger, garlic, and sesame oil. Let the mixture stand for 10 minutes.
2. Grill the tuna in the air fryer for 4 to 7 minutes, or until done to your liking and lightly browned.
3. Make wraps with the grilled tuna, tortillas, mayonnaise, lettuce, and bell pepper. Serve immediately.

FISH AND SEAFOOD CREATIONS

QUICK SHRIMP SCAMPI

Prep time: 5 minutes | **Cook time:** 5 minutes | **Serves** 2 to 4

- 16 to 20 raw large shrimp, peeled, deveined, and tails removed
- ½ cup white wine
- Freshly ground black pepper, to taste
- ¼ cup + 1 tablespoon butter, divided
- 1 clove garlic, sliced
- 1 teaspoon olive oil
- Salt, to taste
- Juice of ½ lemon, to taste
- ¼ cup chopped fresh parsley

1. Marinate the shrimp in the white wine and freshly ground black pepper for at least 30 minutes, or as long as 2 hours in the refrigerator.
2. Preheat the air fryer to 400°F.
3. Melt ¼ cup of butter in a small saucepan over low heat. Add the garlic and let the butter simmer gently, being careful not to burn it.
4. Pour the shrimp and marinade into the air fryer, allowing the marinade to drain through to the bottom. Drizzle the olive oil over the shrimp and season well with salt. Air-fry at 400°F for 3 minutes. Turn the shrimp over (don't shake the basket as the marinade will splash). Pour the garlic butter over the shrimp and air-fry for an additional 2 minutes.
5. Remove the shrimp from the basket and transfer them to a bowl. Squeeze lemon juice over the shrimp and toss with the chopped parsley and the remaining tablespoon of butter. Adjust seasoning with salt if necessary. Serve over rice, pasta, or with some crusty bread.

TROUT AND MINT MIX

Prep time: 5 minutes | **Cooking time:** 16 minutes | **Serves** 4

- 4 rainbow trout
- 1 cup olive oil + 3 tablespoons
- Juice of 1 lemon
- Pinch of salt and black pepper
- 1 cup parsley, chopped
- 3 garlic cloves, minced
- ½ cup mint, chopped
- Zest of 1 lemon
- 1/3 cup pine nuts
- 1 avocado, peeled, pitted, and roughly chopped

1. Pat dry the trout, season with salt and pepper, and rub with 3 tablespoons of olive oil.
2. Place the fish in the air fryer basket and cook for 8 minutes on each side.
3. Divide the cooked fish between plates and drizzle with half of the lemon juice.
4. In a blender, combine the remaining olive oil, lemon juice, parsley, garlic, mint, lemon zest, pine nuts, and avocado. Pulse until well blended.
5. Spread the mint and avocado mixture over the trout and serve.

CHAPTER 6

LEMON-DILL SALMON BURGERS

Prep time: 5 minutes | **Cook time:** 8 minutes | |Serves 4

- 2 (6-ounce) fillets of salmon, finely chopped by hand or in a food processor
- 1 cup fine breadcrumbs
- 1 teaspoon freshly grated lemon zest
- 2 tablespoons chopped fresh dill weed
- 1 teaspoon salt
- Freshly ground black pepper, to taste
- 2 eggs, lightly beaten
- 4 brioche or hamburger buns
- Lettuce, tomato, red onion, avocado, mayonnaise, or mustard, to serve

1. Preheat the air fryer to 400°F.
2. In a bowl, combine the chopped salmon, breadcrumbs, lemon zest, dill, salt, pepper, and eggs. Mix well. Divide the mixture into four portions and shape them into patties. Make an indentation in the center of each patty with your thumb (this helps the burger stay flat as it cooks).
3. Place the patties in the air fryer basket and cook for 4 minutes. Flip the burgers and cook for another 3 to 4 minutes, until golden brown and firm to the touch.
4. Serve on brioche buns with your choice of toppings, such as lettuce, tomato, red onion, avocado, mayonnaise, or mustard.

COCONUT SHRIMP

Prep time: 5 minutes | **Cook time:** 10 minutes | Serves 4

- 1 cup breadcrumbs
- 1 cup dried coconut, unsweetened
- 1 cup almond flour
- Sea salt, to taste
- 2 pounds shrimp, peeled and deveined
- 1 cup egg whites

1. In a mixing bowl, combine the coconut and breadcrumbs.
2. Season lightly with sea salt.
3. In another bowl, add almond flour. In a third bowl, place the egg whites.
4. Preheat your air fryer to 340°F.
5. Dip each shrimp into the flour, then egg whites, then the breadcrumb mixture.
6. Cook the shrimp for 10 minutes, turning halfway through. Serve with your favorite dipping sauce.

CHAPTER 7: SIDE DISHES AND SNACKS

CHAPTER 7

CLASSIC ONION RINGS

Prep time: 10 minutes | **Cook time:** 8 minutes | **Serves** 4

- 1 cup all-purpose flour
- Sea salt and black pepper, to taste
- 1 teaspoon red pepper flakes, crushed
- ½ teaspoon cumin powder
- 1 egg, beaten
- 1 cup breadcrumbs
- 1 medium yellow onion, sliced

1. Preheat the air fryer to 380°F.
2. In a shallow bowl, mix the flour, salt, black pepper, red pepper flakes, and cumin powder.
3. In another shallow bowl, whisk the egg. Place the breadcrumbs in a separate bowl.
4. Dip the onion rings into the flour mixture, then the egg, and finally coat with the breadcrumbs. Place the onion rings in the air fryer basket.
5. Cook the onion rings for about 8 minutes, or until golden brown and cooked through.
6. Bon appétit!

MEDITERRANEAN-STYLE BEET CHIPS

Prep time: 35 minutes | **Cook time:** 30 minutes | **Serves** 4

- 1 pound red and yellow beets, peeled and sliced
- 1 tablespoon olive oil
- Coarse sea salt and ground black pepper, to taste
- 1 teaspoon dried rosemary
- 1 teaspoon dried parsley flakes
- 1 teaspoon garlic powder
- 2 tablespoons scallions, chopped

1. Peel the beets using a vegetable peeler and then slice them into thin, even rounds, about 1/8 inch thick. The thinner the slices, the crispier the chips will be. If you have a mandoline slicer, it can help you achieve uniform thickness.
2. Set your air fryer to 330°F and preheat for about 3 minutes. This will ensure the chips cook evenly right from the start.
3. In a large bowl, toss the beet slices with olive oil until they are evenly coated. Then add the coarse sea salt, ground black pepper, dried rosemary, dried parsley, garlic powder, and chopped scallions. Toss everything together until the beets are evenly seasoned.
4. Lightly coat the air fryer basket with non-stick spray or a small amount of olive oil. Place the seasoned beet slices in the basket in a single layer. You may need to cook the beets in batches depending on the size of your air fryer basket. Avoid overcrowding to ensure the chips get crispy.
5. Cook the beets at 330°F for 30 minutes, shaking the basket every 10 minutes to ensure even cooking and crispiness. Keep an eye on them during the last 5 minutes to make sure they don't burn.
6. The beet chips are done when they are crispy and golden brown. If some slices aren't as crispy as others, you can air fry them for an additional 2-3 minutes.
7. Once the chips are done, remove them from the air fryer and let them cool slightly. Serve immediately as a crunchy snack or side dish.

SIDE DISHES AND SNACKS

TOMATO-CAPRESE CUPS

Prep time: 12 minutes | **Cook time:** 5 minutes | **Makes** 15 pieces

- 1 cup mozzarella-style shreds
- 1 (15-count) package mini phyllo cups
- 1½ tablespoons dried basil
- 15 slices black olives
- 8 small grape tomatoes
- Oil for misting

1. Coarsely chop the vegan mozzarella and press it into the phyllo cups, dividing it evenly.
2. Sprinkle the basil over the cheese.
3. Top each cup with 1 slice of black olive.
4. Halve the tomatoes lengthwise and place 1 tomato half, cut-side down, in each cup.
5. Mist the cups with oil.
6. Arrange the cups in the air fryer basket, ensuring they fit in a single layer.
7. Cook at 390°F for 5 minutes, until the cheese is melted.
8. Serve warm.

SPICED NUTS

Prep time: 5 minutes | **Cook time:** 10 minutes | **Serves** 3 cups

- 1 cup almonds
- 1 cup pecan halves
- 1 cup cashews
- 1 egg white, beaten
- ½ teaspoon cinnamon, ground
- Pinch of cayenne pepper
- ¼ teaspoon ground cloves
- Dash of salt

1. Whisk the egg white with cinnamon, cayenne, cloves, and salt in a bowl.
2. Preheat the air fryer to 300°F.
3. Toss the nuts in the spiced egg white mixture, ensuring they are well-coated.
4. Place the nuts in the air fryer basket and cook for 25 minutes, stirring several times during the cooking process.
5. Bon appétit!

CHAPTER 7

CHEESE BACON-STUFFED MUSHROOMS

Prep time: 10 minutes | **Cook time:** 7 minutes | **Serves** 4

- 1 tablespoon butter
- 6 ounces Pecorino Romano cheese, grated
- 2 tablespoons chives, chopped
- 1 tablespoon minced garlic
- ½ teaspoon cayenne pepper
- Sea salt and ground black pepper, to taste
- 1 pound button mushrooms, stems removed

1. Clean the button mushrooms by gently wiping them with a damp cloth or paper towel. Remove the stems carefully and set the caps aside. You can save the stems for another recipe, like a soup or sauce.
2. In a mixing bowl, melt the butter (you can do this in the microwave or on the stovetop). Add the grated Pecorino Romano cheese, chopped chives, minced garlic, cayenne pepper, sea salt, and ground black pepper to the melted butter. Stir everything together until fully combined into a thick, creamy mixture.
3. Spoon the cheese mixture into each mushroom cap, filling them generously. Be sure to pack the filling in a bit, so it stays inside during cooking.
4. Preheat your air fryer to 400°F for about 3 minutes.
5. Lightly grease the air fryer basket or tray with a little non-stick spray or a brush of olive oil. Place the stuffed mushroom caps in the basket, ensuring they're arranged in a single layer without overlapping.
6. Air fry the mushrooms at 400°F for about 7 minutes. Shake the basket halfway through to ensure even cooking. The mushrooms should be tender, and the cheese filling will be melted and slightly golden on top.
7. Once cooked, remove the mushrooms from the air fryer and let them cool slightly before serving. Enjoy these cheesy, savory bites!

BROCCOLI WITH CHEESE & OLIVES

Prep time: 5 minutes | **Cook time:** 15 minutes | **Serves** 4

- 2 pounds broccoli florets
- ¼ cup Parmesan cheese, shaved
- 2 teaspoons lemon zest, grated
- ⅓ cup Kalamata olives, halved and pitted
- ½ teaspoon ground black pepper
- 1 teaspoon sea salt
- 2 tablespoons olive oil

1. Boil water in a pan and cook the broccoli for 4 minutes.
2. Drain the broccoli.
3. Toss the broccoli with olive oil, salt, and pepper.
4. Place the broccoli in the air fryer basket and cook at 400°F for 15 minutes, tossing twice during the cooking time.
5. Move to a serving bowl and toss in lemon zest, olives, and cheese.

SIDE DISHES AND SNACKS

GARLIC & GINGER SNOW PEAS

Prep time: 5 minutes | **Cook time:** 8 minutes | **Serves** 4

- 2 cups snow peas, trimmed
- 1 teaspoon olive oil
- 1 teaspoon pepper
- 1 teaspoon sea salt
- 1 tablespoon rice vinegar
- 1 tablespoon tamari sauce
- 2 cloves garlic, minced
- 3 inches of ginger root, minced

1. Wash the snow peas with cold running water, then trim them.
2. Clean the ginger and garlic with water, then slice them into small pieces. Set aside.
3. In a large bowl, combine the tamari sauce, rice vinegar, salt, pepper, and olive oil.
4. Mix in the minced ginger and garlic.
5. Add the snow peas and toss to coat.
6. Let the peas marinate for about an hour.
7. Preheat the air fryer to 380°F for 2 minutes.
8. Transfer the marinated snow peas into the air fryer basket and cook for 4 minutes.
9. Toss the peas and cook for an additional 4 minutes.
10. Bon appétit!

ARTICHOKE BALLS

Prep time: 26 minutes | **Cook time:** 10 minutes | **Makes** 15 balls

- 1 (14-ounce) can artichoke hearts, drained
- 1 cup panko breadcrumbs
- 1 tablespoon extra-virgin olive oil
- 1 teaspoon vegan Worcestershire sauce
- 2 tablespoons grated Parmesan-style topping
- 1 cup nut milk (of choice)
- 1 tablespoon thinly sliced green onions

1. Using your hands, smash the artichoke hearts and mix them with all the ingredients to make a stiff mixture.
2. Shape the mixture into 1 tablespoon-sized balls.
3. Place the artichoke balls in the air fryer basket, keeping them close together but not touching.
4. Cook at 390°F for 10 minutes.
5. Serve warm or at room temperature.

CHAPTER 7

PARMESAN ASPARAGUS FRIES

Prep time: 5 minutes | **Cook time:** 10 minutes | **Serves** 5

- 1 pound asparagus spears
- ¼ cup almond flour
- Salt and pepper, to taste
- 2 eggs, beaten
- ½ cup Parmesan cheese, grated
- 1 cup pork rinds, crushed

1. Preheat the air fryer to 380°F.
2. Combine the pork rinds and Parmesan cheese in a small bowl and season with salt and pepper.
3. Dip half of the asparagus spears into almond flour, then into the eggs, and finally coat them in the pork rind mixture.
4. Place the asparagus spears on the air fryer basket and cook for 10 minutes.
5. Repeat with the remaining spears.

CRISPY ZUCCHINI FRIES

Prep time: 15 minutes | **Cook time:** 10 minutes | **Serves** 4

- 1 pound zucchini, cut into sticks
- 1 egg, whisked
- ¼ cup Parmesan cheese, grated
- ½ cup breadcrumbs
- 1 teaspoon garlic powder
- ½ teaspoon onion powder
- Sea salt and ground black pepper, to taste

1. Preheat the air fryer to 390°F.
2. Toss the zucchini sticks with the Parmesan, breadcrumbs, garlic powder, onion powder, salt, and pepper.
3. Arrange the zucchini sticks in a single layer in the air fryer basket.
4. Cook at 390°F for about 10 minutes, shaking the basket halfway through the cooking time. Work in batches if necessary.
5. Bon appétit!

SIDE DISHES AND SNACKS

CHEDDAR-OLIVE NUGGETS

Prep time: 20 minutes | **Cook time:** 20 minutes | **Makes** 24–26 nuggets

- 1 (7-ounce) jar pimento-stuffed green olives, drained and blotted dry
- 1 cup Monterey Jack & Cheddar-style shreds
- 1 cup self-rising flour
- 1½ tablespoons all-vegetable shortening
- 3 tablespoons almond milk
- Oil for misting
- Strawberry jam (optional, for dipping)

1. Drain the olives and blot them dry with paper towels.
2. Chop the cheese and place it in a medium bowl.
3. Add the flour to the cheese and mix together with your hands.
4. Work the shortening into the mixture until it's well blended.
5. Add the almond milk and mix until a dough forms.
6. Take 1½ teaspoons of dough for each olive, roll it into a ball, and then flatten it into a disc about 2½ inches in diameter.
7. Place an olive in the center of each disc, wrap the dough around the olive, and pinch the edges to seal.
8. Mist the nuggets with oil and place them in the air fryer basket in a single layer.
9. Cook at 390°F for 13–15 minutes, until golden and brown.
10. Repeat the process for the remaining nuggets.
11. Serve with strawberry jam for dipping, if desired.

SPICY AND STICKY BRUSSELS SPROUTS

Prep time: 15 minutes | **Cook time:** 10 minutes | **Serves** 4

- 1 pound Brussels sprouts, trimmed
- 2 tablespoons sesame oil
- 2 tablespoons agave syrup
- 2 tablespoons rice wine
- 1 teaspoon chili flakes
- 1 teaspoon garlic powder
- ½ teaspoon paprika
- Sea salt and ground black pepper, to taste

1. Toss the Brussels sprouts with the sesame oil, agave syrup, rice wine, chili flakes, garlic powder, paprika, salt, and pepper.
2. Arrange the Brussels sprouts in the air fryer basket.
3. Cook at 380°F for 10 minutes, shaking the basket halfway through the cooking time.
4. Serve warm and enjoy!

CHAPTER 8: VEGAN AND VEGETARIAN MEALS

VEGAN AND VEGETARIAN MEALS

HOT SPICY FALAFEL

Prep time: 20 minutes | **Cook time:** 15 minutes | **Serves** 4

- 1½ cups chickpeas, canned or boiled
- 1 shallot, diced
- 2 cloves garlic, minced
- 2 tablespoons olive oil
- ¼ cup parsley leaves, chopped
- 1 teaspoon red chili powder
- ½ teaspoon cumin powder
- ½ teaspoon mustard powder
- 1 teaspoon cayenne pepper
- Sea salt and ground black pepper, to taste

1. Pulse the chickpeas, shallot, garlic, olive oil, parsley, and all the spices in a food processor until well incorporated.
2. Shape the mixture into balls and place them in the air fryer basket, lightly greased.
3. Cook the falafel at 380°F for about 15 minutes, shaking the basket occasionally to ensure even cooking.
4. Serve in pita bread with toppings of your choice.

CREAMED SPINACH

Prep time: 10 minutes | **Cook time:** 15 minutes | **Serves** 4

- Vegetable oil spray
- 1 (10-ounce) package frozen spinach, thawed and squeezed dry
- ½ cup chopped onion
- 2 cloves garlic, minced
- 4 ounces cream cheese, diced
- ½ teaspoon ground nutmeg
- 1 teaspoon kosher salt
- 1 teaspoon black pepper
- ½ cup grated Parmesan cheese

1. Spray a 6 × 3-inch round heatproof pan with vegetable oil spray.
2. In a medium bowl, combine the spinach, onion, garlic, cream cheese, nutmeg, salt, and pepper. Transfer to the prepared pan.
3. Place the pan in the air fryer basket. Set the air fryer to 350°F for 10 minutes. Open and stir to thoroughly combine the cream cheese and spinach.
4. Sprinkle the Parmesan cheese on top. Set the air fryer to 400°F for 5 minutes, or until the cheese has melted and browned.

CHAPTER 8

SMASHED FRIED BABY POTATOES

Prep time: 5 minutes | **Cook time:** 18 minutes | Serves 3 to 4

- 1½ pounds baby red or baby Yukon gold potatoes
- ¼ cup butter, melted
- 1 teaspoon olive oil
- ½ teaspoon paprika
- 1 teaspoon dried parsley
- Salt and freshly ground black pepper
- 2 scallions, finely chopped

1. Bring a large pot of salted water to a boil. Add the potatoes and boil for 18 minutes or until the potatoes are fork-tender.
2. Drain the potatoes and transfer them to a cutting board to cool slightly. Spray or brush the bottom of a drinking glass with a little oil. Smash or flatten the potatoes by pressing the glass down on each potato slowly. Try not to completely flatten the potato or smash it so hard that it breaks apart.
3. Combine the melted butter, olive oil, paprika, and parsley together.
4. Pre-heat the air fryer to 400°F.
5. Spray the bottom of the air fryer basket with oil and transfer one layer of the smashed potatoes into the basket. Brush with some of the butter mixture and season generously with salt and freshly ground black pepper.
6. Air-fry at 400°F for 10 minutes. Carefully flip the potatoes over and air-fry for an additional 8 minutes until crispy and lightly browned.
7. Keep the potatoes warm in a 170°F oven or tent with aluminum foil while you cook the second batch. Sprinkle minced scallions over the potatoes and serve warm.

ROASTED STUFFED PEPPERS

Prep time: 15 minutes | **Cook time:** 25 minutes | Serves 2

- ½ pound lentils or plant-based crumbles (like lentil, tempeh, or vegan ground «beef» alternative)
- 2 teaspoons olive oil
- 2 tablespoons diced scallion
- 2 tablespoons fresh parsley, chopped
- ¼ teaspoon granulated garlic
- ¼ teaspoon salt
- ½ cup cooked white or brown rice
- ½ cup marinara sauce
- 2 green bell peppers
- 2 tablespoons dairy-free shredded mozzarella cheese (optional for topping)

1. In a skillet, heat the olive oil over medium heat and sauté the lentils or plant-based crumbles for 7–10 minutes until browned and heated through. (If using lentils, be sure they are pre-cooked.)
2. Drain any excess moisture and transfer the lentils or crumbles to a large bowl. Stir in the scallions, parsley, granulated garlic, and salt.
3. Add the cooked rice and marinara sauce to the bowl and stir to combine.
4. Cut the tops off the bell peppers, remove the seeds, and stuff them with the lentil and rice mixture.
5. Place the stuffed peppers in the air fryer basket and roast for 10 minutes.
6. Add the dairy-free mozzarella cheese on top of the peppers and roast for an additional 5 minutes, or until the cheese is melted and bubbly.
7. Serve and enjoy!

VEGAN AND VEGETARIAN MEALS

LEMON GARLICKY CABBAGE

Prep time: 10 minutes | **Cook time:** 7 minutes | **Serves** 4

- 1 pound cabbage, cut into wedges
- 2 tablespoons olive oil
- 1 teaspoon garlic, minced
- Kosher salt and freshly ground black pepper, to taste
- ¼ teaspoon cumin powder
- ½ teaspoon bay leaf, crushed
- 2 tablespoons fresh lemon juice
- 1 teaspoon red pepper flakes, crushed

1. Toss the cabbage wedges with olive oil, garlic, salt, pepper, cumin, bay leaf, lemon juice, and red pepper flakes.
2. Cook the cabbage wedges in the air fryer at 350°F for 7 minutes, shaking the basket halfway through.
3. Taste and adjust the seasonings if necessary.
4. Bon appétit!

GREEK-STYLE VEGAN BURGERS

Prep time: 20 minutes | **Cook time:** 15 minutes | **Serves** 4

- 1 tablespoon ground chia seeds
- 14 ounces canned chickpeas, rinsed and drained
- ¼ cup fresh coriander, chopped
- ¼ cup fresh scallions, chopped
- 1 tablespoon rosemary
- 1 tablespoon thyme
- 1 tablespoon basil
- 2 garlic cloves, peeled
- ½ teaspoon ground cumin
- Sea salt and ground black pepper, to taste
- 2 tablespoons fresh lemon juice

1. To make a flax egg, soak the ground chia seeds in 2 tablespoons of water for 15 minutes.
2. Blend all the ingredients, including the chia egg, until well combined.
3. Shape the mixture into patties and place them in a lightly greased air fryer basket.
4. Air fry the patties at 380°F for about 15 minutes, turning them halfway through.
5. Bon appétit!

CHAPTER 8

CHILE-CHEESE CORNBREAD WITH CORN

Prep time: 10 minutes | **Cook time:** 15 minutes | **Serves** 6

- 2 large eggs
- ¼ cup whole milk
- 1 (8.5-ounce) package corn muffin mix
- 1 cup corn kernels
- ½ cup grated cheddar cheese
- 1 (4-ounce) can diced mild green chiles, undrained
- Vegetable oil spray
- Parchment paper

1. In a medium bowl, whisk together the eggs and milk. Add the muffin mix and stir until the batter is smooth. Stir in the corn, cheese, and undrained chiles.
2. Spray a 3-cup Bundt pan with vegetable oil spray. Line the pan with parchment paper. (To do this, cut a circle of parchment about 1 inch larger in diameter than the top of the pan. Fold the parchment in half and cut a hole in the middle to accommodate the center of the Bundt pan. Place the parchment in the pan; trim any excess parchment from around the top.)
3. Pour the batter into the prepared pan. Place the pan in the air fryer basket. Set the air fryer to 350°F for 15 minutes.
4. Allow the bread to rest in the closed air fryer for 10 minutes before serving.

FRIED GREEN TOMATOES

Prep time: 15 minutes | **Cook time:** 6 to 8 minutes | **Serves** 4

- 4 medium green tomatoes
- ⅓ cup all-purpose flour
- 2 egg whites
- ¼ cup almond milk
- 1 cup ground almonds
- ½ cup panko bread crumbs
- 2 teaspoons olive oil
- 1 teaspoon paprika
- 1 clove garlic, minced

1. Rinse the tomatoes and pat dry. Cut the tomatoes into ½-inch slices, discarding the thinner ends.
2. Put the flour on a plate. In a shallow bowl, beat the egg whites with the almond milk until frothy. On another plate, combine the almonds, bread crumbs, olive oil, paprika, and garlic and mix well.
3. Dip the tomato slices into the flour, then into the egg white mixture, then into the almond mixture to coat.
4. Place four of the coated tomato slices in the air fryer basket. Air fry for 6 to 8 minutes or until the tomato coating is crisp and golden brown. Repeat with remaining tomato slices and serve immediately.

VEGAN AND VEGETARIAN MEALS

CRISPY BAKED GREEN BEANS

Prep time: 5 minutes | **Cook time:** 10 minutes | **Makes** 2 cups

- 2 cups fresh green beans
- 2 tablespoons olive oil
- 2 teaspoons granulated garlic
- ½ teaspoon salt
- ½ teaspoon lemon pepper

1. Trim the ends of the green beans and snap them in half.
2. Toss the beans in olive oil, granulated garlic, salt, and lemon pepper to coat.
3. Place the green beans in the air fryer basket and cook for 10 minutes, stopping halfway to toss them.
4. Return the basket to the air fryer to cook for the remaining 5 minutes, or until the beans are fork-tender.

ROSEMARY & CHEESE-ROASTED RED POTATOES

Prep time: 10 minutes | **Cook time:** 15 minutes | **Serves** 4

- 4 cups quartered baby red potatoes
- 3 tablespoons extra-virgin olive oil
- 2 teaspoons chopped fresh rosemary
- ¼ teaspoon garlic powder
- Kosher salt and black pepper, to taste
- ¼ cup plus 1 tablespoon finely grated Parmesan cheese
- ¼ cup chopped fresh parsley

1. In a large bowl, toss together the potatoes, olive oil, rosemary, garlic powder, salt, and pepper to taste, and ¼ cup of the Parmesan until the potatoes are well coated.
2. Place the seasoned potatoes in the air fryer basket. Set the air fryer to 400°F for 15 minutes, or until potatoes are tender when pierced with a fork.
3. Transfer the potatoes to a serving platter or bowl. Toss with the remaining 1 tablespoon Parmesan and the parsley.

CHAPTER 8

HERB-ROASTED VEGETABLES

Prep time: 10 minutes | **Cook time:** 14 to 18 minutes | **Serves** 4

- 1 red bell pepper, sliced
- 1 (8-ounce) package sliced mushrooms
- 1 cup green beans, cut into 2-inch pieces
- 1/3 cup diced red onion
- 3 garlic cloves, sliced
- 1 teaspoon olive oil
- ½ teaspoon dried basil
- ½ teaspoon dried tarragon

1. In a medium bowl, mix the red bell pepper, mushrooms, green beans, red onion, and garlic. Drizzle with the olive oil. Toss to coat.
2. Add the herbs and toss again.
3. Place the vegetables in the air fryer basket. Roast for 14 to 18 minutes, or until tender. Serve immediately.

BREADED ZUCCHINI SLICES

Prep time: 15 minutes | **Cook time:** 10 minutes | **Serves** 4

- 1 pound zucchini, sliced
- 1 tablespoon chia seeds, ground
- ½ cup crackers, crushed
- 2 tablespoons olive oil
- 1 teaspoon cayenne pepper
- Kosher salt and ground black pepper, to taste

1. Preheat your air fryer to 390°F.
2. Mix the chia seeds, crushed crackers, cayenne pepper, salt, and pepper in a bowl.
3. Dip the zucchini slices into the mixture, coating them evenly.
4. Arrange the zucchini slices in a single layer in the air fryer basket.
5. Cook the zucchini slices for about 10 minutes at 390°F, shaking the basket halfway through.
6. Bon appétit!

CHAPTER 9: DELICIOUS DESSERTS

CHAPTER 9

PUMPKIN PIE ROLL-UPS

Prep time: 7 minutes | **Cook time:** 10 minutes | **Makes** 4 rolls

- 4 egg roll wrappers
- 1 small can pumpkin pie filling
- Water, for brushing
- 2 tablespoons butter, melted

1. Lay one egg roll wrapper in front of you with a point facing toward you.
2. Scoop 2 to 3 tablespoons of pie filling into the center of the wrapper, and use your hands to form it into a tube shape that runs lengthwise along the edge of the wrapper.
3. Fold the point of the wrapper nearest you over the filling, and pull gently to compact it even more.
4. Fold the sides in, and roll the wrapper away from you until you have just a couple inches left.
5. Moisten your finger with water, and run it along the edge of the wrapper, then finish rolling the wrapper up, smoothing the seam with your finger to help hold it in place.
6. Repeat with the remaining filling and wrappers.
7. Place the prepared roll-ups in the fryer basket, and brush with the melted butter.
8. Bake for 10 minutes, turning the roll-ups over halfway through the cooking time, until golden and crispy. Serve warm.

BANANAS FOSTER

Prep time: 5 minutes | **Cook time:** 7 minutes | **Serves** 2

- 1 tablespoon unsalted butter
- 2 teaspoons dark brown sugar
- 1 banana, peeled and halved lengthwise and then crosswise
- 2 tablespoons chopped pecans
- ⅛ teaspoon ground cinnamon
- 2 tablespoons light rum
- Vanilla ice cream, for serving

1. In a 6 × 3-inch round heatproof pan, combine the butter and brown sugar. Place the pan in the air fryer basket. Set the air fryer to 350°F for 2 minutes, or until the butter and sugar are melted. Swirl to combine.
2. Add the banana pieces and pecans, turning the bananas to coat. Set the air fryer to 350°F for 5 minutes, turning the banana pieces halfway through the cooking time. Sprinkle with the cinnamon.
3. Remove the pan from the air fryer and place on an unlit stovetop for safety. Add the rum to the pan, swirling to combine it with the butter mixture. Carefully light the sauce with a long-reach lighter. Spoon the flaming sauce over the banana pieces until the flames die out.
4. Serve the warm bananas and sauce over vanilla ice cream.

DELICIOUS DESSERTS

GRILLED PLANTAIN BOATS

Prep time: 10 minutes | **Cook time:** 7 minutes | Serves 2

- 2 plantains, peeled
- ½ cup coconut, shredded
- 1 tablespoon coconut oil
- 4 tablespoons brown sugar
- ½ teaspoon cinnamon powder
- ½ teaspoon cardamom powder
- 4 tablespoons raisins

1. In the peel, slice your plantains lengthwise, making sure not to slice all the way through the plantains.
2. Divide the remaining ingredients between the plantain pockets.
3. Place the plantain boats in the Air Fryer grill pan. Cook at 395°F for 7 minutes.
4. Eat with a spoon and enjoy!

BLUEBERRY-CREAM CHEESE BREAD PUDDING

Prep time: 15 minutes | **Cook time:** 70 minutes | Serves 6

- 1 cup light cream or half-and-half
- 4 large eggs
- ⅓ cup plus 3 tablespoons granulated sugar
- 1 teaspoon pure lemon extract
- 4 cups cubed croissants (4 to 5 croissants)
- 1 cup blueberries
- 4 ounces cream cheese, cut into small cubes

1. In a large bowl, combine the cream, eggs, the 1/3 cup sugar, and the extract. Whisk until well combined. Add the cubed croissants, blueberries, and cream cheese. Toss gently until everything is thoroughly combined; set aside.
2. Place a 3-cup Bundt pan in the air fryer basket. Preheat the air fryer to 400°F.
3. Sprinkle the remaining 3 tablespoons sugar in the bottom of the hot pan. Set the air fryer to 400°F for 10 minutes, or until the sugar caramelizes. Tip the pan to spread the caramel evenly across the bottom of the pan.
4. Remove the pan from the air fryer and pour in the bread mixture, distributing it evenly across the pan. Place the pan in the air fryer basket. Set the air fryer to 350°F for 60 minutes, or until the custard is set in the middle. Let stand for 10 minutes before unmolding onto a serving plate.

CHAPTER 9

MINI MONKEY ROLLS

Prep time: 25 minutes | **Cook time:** 20 minutes | **Serves** 4

- 12 ounces refrigerated dinner roll dough
- ½ cup brown sugar
- 1 teaspoon ground cinnamon
- ¼ cup almonds, chopped
- ¼ cup butter, melted

1. Spritz muffin cups with a nonstick cooking spray.
2. Separate the dough into biscuits. In a shallow bowl, thoroughly combine the sugar, cinnamon, almonds, and butter.
3. Roll the biscuits over the sugar/cinnamon mixture. Divide them between muffin cups.
4. Bake the mini monkey rolls at 340°F for about 20 minutes or until golden brown. Turn them upside down and serve.

DARK CHOCOLATE OATMEAL COOKIES

Prep time: 10 minutes | **Cook time:** 13 minutes | **Makes** 30 cookies

- 3 tablespoons unsalted butter
- 2 ounces dark chocolate, chopped
- ½ cup packed brown sugar
- 2 egg whites
- 1 teaspoon pure vanilla extract
- 1 cup quick-cooking oatmeal
- ½ cup whole-wheat pastry flour
- ½ teaspoon baking soda
- ¼ cup dried cranberries

1. In a medium metal bowl, mix the butter and dark chocolate. Bake in the air fryer for 1 to 3 minutes, or until the butter and chocolate melt. Stir until smooth.
2. Beat in the brown sugar, egg whites, and vanilla until smooth.
3. Stir in the oatmeal, pastry flour, and baking soda.
4. Stir in the cranberries. Form the dough into about 30 (1-inch) balls. Bake the dough balls, in batches of 8, in the air fryer basket for 7 to 10 minutes, or until set.
5. Carefully remove the cookies from the air fryer and cool on a wire rack. Repeat with the remaining dough balls.

DELICIOUS DESSERTS

S'MORES POCKETS

Prep time: 2 minutes | **Cook time:** 5 minutes | **Serves** 6

- 12 sheets phyllo dough, thawed
- 1½ cups butter, melted
- ¾ cup graham cracker crumbs
- 1 (7-ounce) Giant Hershey's® milk chocolate bar
- 12 marshmallows, cut in half

1. Place one sheet of the phyllo on a large cutting board. Keep the rest of the phyllo sheets covered with a slightly damp, clean kitchen towel. Brush the phyllo sheet generously with some melted butter. Place a second phyllo sheet on top of the first and brush it with more butter. Repeat with one more phyllo sheet until you have a stack of 3 phyllo sheets with butter brushed between the layers. Cover the phyllo sheets with one-quarter of the graham cracker crumbs, leaving a 1-inch border on one of the short ends of the rectangle. Cut the phyllo sheets lengthwise into 3 strips.
2. Take 2 of the strips and crisscross them to form a cross with the empty borders at the top and to the left. Place 2 of the chocolate rectangles in the center of the cross. Place 4 of the marshmallow halves on top of the chocolate. Now fold the pocket together by folding the bottom phyllo strip up over the chocolate and marshmallows. Then fold the right side over, then the top strip down and finally the left side over. Brush all the edges generously with melted butter to seal shut. Repeat with the next three sheets of phyllo, until all the sheets have been used. You will be able to make 2 pockets with every second batch because you will have an extra graham cracker crumb strip from the previous set of sheets.
3. Preheat the air fryer to 350°F.
4. Transfer 3 pockets at a time to the air fryer basket. Air-fry at 350°F for 4 to 5 minutes, until the phyllo dough is light brown in color. Flip the pockets over halfway through the cooking process. Repeat with the remaining 3 pockets.
5. Serve warm.

EASY FUDGE BROWNIE

Prep time: 25 minutes | **Cook time:** 20 minutes | **Serves** 6

- ½ cup butter, melted
- ½ cup granulated sugar
- 2 eggs, whisked
- ¾ cup self-raising flour
- ¼ cup cocoa powder
- 1 teaspoon vanilla extract
- ½ cup chocolate chips

1. Start by preheating your Air Fryer to 340°F. Now, spritz the sides and bottom of a baking pan with a nonstick cooking spray.
2. In a mixing bowl, beat the melted butter and sugar until fluffy. Next, fold in the eggs and beat again until well combined.
3. After that, add in the remaining ingredients. Mix until everything is well incorporated.
4. Bake your brownie in the preheated Air Fryer for approximately 20 minutes. Enjoy!

CHAPTER 9

GLAZED CHERRY TURNOVERS

Prep time: 10 minutes | **Cook time:** 56 minutes | **Serves** 8

- 2 sheets frozen puff pastry, thawed
- 1 (21-ounce) can premium cherry pie filling
- 2 teaspoons ground cinnamon
- 1 egg, beaten
- 1 cup sliced almonds
- 1 cup powdered sugar
- 2 tablespoons milk

1. Roll a sheet of puff pastry out into a square that is approximately 10 inches by 10 inches. Cut this large square into quarters.
2. Mix the cherry pie filling and cinnamon together in a bowl. Spoon ¼ cup of the cherry filling into the center of each puff pastry square. Brush the perimeter of the pastry square with the egg wash. Fold one corner of the puff pastry over the cherry pie filling towards the opposite corner, forming a triangle. Seal the two edges of the pastry together with the tip of a fork, making a design with the tines. Brush the top of the turnovers with the egg wash and sprinkle sliced almonds over each one. Repeat these steps with the second sheet of puff pastry. You should have eight turnovers at the end.
3. Preheat the air fryer to 370°F.
4. Air-fry two turnovers at a time for 14 minutes, carefully turning them over halfway through the cooking time.
5. While the turnovers are cooking, make the glaze by whisking the powdered sugar and milk together in a small bowl until smooth. Let the glaze sit for a minute so the sugar can absorb the milk. If the consistency is still too thick to drizzle, add a little more milk, a drop at a time, and stir until smooth.
6. Let the cooked cherry turnovers sit for at least 10 minutes. Then drizzle the glaze over each turnover in a zigzag motion. Serve warm or at room temperature.

APPENDIX 1: MEASUREMENT CONVERSION CHART

MEASUREMENT CONVERSION CHART

VOLUME EQUIVALENTS (DRY)

US STANDARD	METRIC (APPROXIMATE)
1/8 teaspoon	0.5 mL
1/4 teaspoon	1 mL
1/2 teaspoon	2 mL
3/4 teaspoon	4 mL
1 teaspoon	5 mL
1 tablespoon	15 mL
1/4 cup	59 mL
1/2 cup	118 mL
3/4 cup	177 mL
1 cup	235 mL
2 cups	475 mL
3 cups	700 mL
4 cups	1 L

VOLUME EQUIVALENTS (LIQUID)

US STANDARD	US STANDARD (OUNCES)	METRIC (APPROXIMATE)
2 tablespoons	1 fl.oz.	30 mL
1/4 cup	2 fl.oz.	60 mL
1/2 cup	4 fl.oz.	120 mL
1 cup	8 fl.oz.	240 mL
1 1/2 cup	12 fl.oz.	355 mL
2 cups or 1 pint	16 fl.oz.	475 mL
4 cups or 1 quart	32 fl.oz.	1 L
1 gallon	128 fl.oz.	4 L

WEIGHT EQUIVALENTS

US STANDARD	METRIC (APPROXIMATE)
1 ounce	28 g
2 ounces	57 g
5 ounces	142 g
10 ounces	284 g
15 ounces	425 g
16 ounces (1 pound)	455 g
1.5 pounds	680 g
2 pounds	907 g

TEMPERATURES EQUIVALENTS

FAHRENHEIT (F)	CELSIUS (C) (APPROXIMATE)
225 °F	107 °C
250 °F	120 °C
275 °F	135 °C
300 °F	150 °C
325 °F	160 °C
350 °F	180 °C
375 °F	190 °C
400 °F	205 °C
425 °F	220 °C
450 °F	235 °C
475 °F	245 °C
500 °F	260 °C

APPENDIX 2: THE DIRTY DOZEN AND CLEAN FIFTEEN

The Dirty Dozen and Clean Fifteen

The Environmental Working Group (EWG) is a nonprofit, nonpartisan organization dedicated to protecting human health and the environment Its mission is to empower people to live healthier lives in a healthier environment. This organization publishes an annual list of the twelve kinds of produce, in sequence, that have the highest amount of pesticide residue-the Dirty Dozen-as well as a list of the fifteen kinds ofproduce that have the least amount of pesticide residue-the Clean Fifteen.

THE DIRTY DOZEN

- The 2016 Dirty Dozen includes the following produce. These are considered among the year's most important produce to buy organic:

Strawberries	Spinach
Apples	Tomatoes
Nectarines	Bell peppers
Peaches	Cherry tomatoes
Celery	Cucumbers
Grapes	Kale/collard greens
Cherries	Hot peppers

- The Dirty Dozen list contains two additional itemskale/collard greens and hot peppers-because they tend to contain trace levels of highly hazardous pesticides.

THE CLEAN FIFTEEN

- The least critical to buy organically are the Clean Fifteen list. The following are on the 2016 list:

Avocados	Papayas
Corn	Kiw
Pineapples	Eggplant
Cabbage	Honeydew
Sweet peas	Grapefruit
Onions	Cantaloupe
Asparagus	Cauliflower
Mangos	

- Some of the sweet corn sold in the United States are made from genetically engineered (GE) seedstock. Buy organic varieties of these crops to avoid GE produce.

APPENDIX 3: INDEX

A

agave syrup 47

almond flour 25, 40, 46

almond milk 47, 52

almonds 43, 52, 58, 60

apple cider vinegar 13, 17

artichoke hearts 45

asparagus spears 46

avocado 25, 36, 39, 40

B

bacon 1, 19, 33

beef flank steak 32

beef shoulder 30

blueberries 57

breadcrumbs 12, 23, 24, 25, 27, 36, 37, 38, 40, 42, 45, 46

broccoli 9, 44

brown sugar 56, 57, 58

Brussels sprouts 47

buckwheat flour 16

C

cabbage 14, 51

capicola 20

cashews 43

cauliflower 33

chia seeds 51, 54

chicken breasts 23, 24, 27

chicken fillets 18, 27

chicken thighs 26, 28

chicken wings 25, 28

chickpeas 10, 49, 51

chuck roast 34

cilantro 14, 21, 38

cod fillet 38

cod fish fillets 36

coleslaw 36

cranberries 58

E

egg 11, 12, 14, 16, 17, 18, 19, 20, 23, 24, 27, 37, 40, 42, 43, 46, 51, 52, 56, 58, 60

G

grapes 13

Greek yogurt 12, 13

green beans 53, 54

guacamole 38

H

halibut 37

APPENDIX 3: INDEX

ham 9, 24

hamburger buns 37, 40

heavy cream 17, 18, 19

J

jalapeño pepper 11, 28

M

maple syrup 33

marshmallows 59

mayonnaise 9, 20, 38, 40

monkfish fillets 36

mushrooms 14, 21, 26, 31, 44, 54

N

nutmeg 26, 37, 49

O

onion flakes 9

oregano 18

P

paprika 13, 18, 23, 26, 33, 34, 37, 47, 50, 52

peas 45

pecans 21, 56

pineapple 26

pork cutlets 33

pork loin chops 32

pork rinds 24, 46

pork tenderloin 34

pumpkin 56

R

rainbow trout 39

raisins 21, 57

ribeye steak 30, 31

rosemary 30, 42, 51, 53

S

salmon fillet 11

salmon strips 37

shrimp 14, 39, 40

T

tarragon 54

tenderloin steaks 31

teriyaki sauce 26

tortillas 38

tuna 19, 38

turkey 23, 25, 26

turkey breast 23

V

vanilla extract 58, 59

W

wine 39, 47

Worcestershire sauce 45

Z

zucchini 46, 54

Hey there!

Wow, can you believe we've reached the end of this culinary journey together? I'm truly thrilled and filled with joy as I think back on all the recipes we've shared and the flavors we've discovered. This experience, blending a bit of tradition with our own unique twists, has been a journey of love for good food. And knowing you've been out there, giving these dishes a try, has made this adventure incredibly special to me.

Even though we're turning the last page of this book, I hope our conversation about all things delicious doesn't have to end. I cherish your thoughts, your experiments, and yes, even those moments when things didn't go as planned. Every piece of feedback you share is invaluable, helping to enrich this experience for us all.

I'd be so grateful if you could take a moment to share your thoughts with me, be it through a review on Amazon or any other place you feel comfortable expressing yourself online. Whether it's praise, constructive criticism, or even an idea for how we might do things differently in the future, your input is what truly makes this journey meaningful.

This book is a piece of my heart, offered to you with all the love and enthusiasm I have for cooking. But it's your engagement and your words that elevate it to something truly extraordinary.

Thank you from the bottom of my heart for being such an integral part of this culinary adventure. Your openness to trying new things and sharing your experiences has been the greatest gift.

Catch you later,

Amy G. Mattison

Printed in Great Britain
by Amazon